Leadership *in a* Lost Generation

Leadership Principles for Today from the Life of Moses

Barry Bowater

◆ FriesenPress

One Printers Way
Altona, MB R0G 0B0
Canada

www.friesenpress.com

Edited by Wendy Bowater

As an Adizes Associate for the past twelve years, I have benefited greatly from the teaching of Dr. Ichak Adizes. Many of the principles illustrated in the book are inspired by his teaching including the frequent use of the Lifecycle both from a corporate and personal perspective.

ISBN
978-1-03-919291-1 (Hardcover)
978-1-03-919290-4 (Paperback)
978-1-03-919292-8 (eBook)

1. BUSINESS & ECONOMICS, LEADERSHIP

Distributed to the trade by The Ingram Book Company

Leadership *in a* Lost Generation

TABLE OF CONTENTS

"If people can't see what God is doing,
they stumble all over themselves;
But when they attend to what he reveals,
they are most blessed"
(*The Message,* Prov. 29:18).

To Christian Leaders:
God risks His reputation to live His life in ours.
How then should we live as ambassadors for Christ?

All Scripture verses are quoted from the
New International Version, unless otherwise noted.
Holy Bible, New International Version.
NIV Copyright 1973, 1978, 1984, 2011 by Biblica Inc

INTRODUCTION

OVER FORTY YEARS AGO, I WROTE A Bible study on the character-istics of leadership from the life of Moses, and it has served me well both personally and with others, as I have shared it many times. The more I studied the life of Moses, the more I realized that he was born into an environment that believed he was a leader. He became a leader as a result of his personality and the circumstances that evolved based on a purpose that was assigned to him by others. To become the leader that God wanted him to be, he had to learn the significance of his relationship with God because it was only that relationship that would get him through the tough times with a sense of contentment and satisfaction.

The Israelites had been in Egypt for 430 years before Moses was called by God to lead them out and begin a journey to the Promised Land. In the latter part of their stay in Egypt, the Israelite numbers were increasing rapidly, and they became a threat to the Egyptian leadership, resulting in them being forced into slavery. At the time of Moses's birth, Pharaoh had ordered that every Hebrew male child born should be killed. Moses' faithful parents hid Moses in a basket and placed him in the reeds of the Nile River, trusting God to preserve his life.

The story of Moses's rescue at the hand of Pharaoh's daughter is a miraculous indication of how God controls the circumstances in our lives that allow us to fulfill the purpose that He has planned for us, assuming that we trust Him with all our hearts.

Moses's journey through life is a study in leadership as he faced both opportunity and threat while leading upwards of 3 million people on a journey that should have taken two years, but lasted forty. During this time, the first generation of the Exodus died in the desert as a result of their lack of trust. This generation of Israelites was not lost from a geographical perspective because God led the way, but they were certainly lost spiritually.

The parallel between their generation and ours should not be lost on us. The Israelites had become used to the Egyptian way of life, its culture and religious beliefs, and for many, the faith of their forefathers had become a distant memory. Today, approximately one third of the world's population identify themselves as Christians, and for many of these, the definition would include a cultural identity as well as nominalism.

The purpose of this book is to define Christian leadership from God's perspective as it was demonstrated through the life of Moses. Moses is known as one of the greatest leaders in the Bible, but his strength, wisdom, and courage came through his ever-maturing relationship with God that was described in Exodus 33:11 as, "God would speak to Moses face to face, as one speaks to a friend."

Should effective Christian leadership be any different today? The challenges that Moses faced are very similar to what we face today. The Israelites were a lost generation seeking a promise that could only be found in a relationship with God. We are living in a world order led by humanistic ideals and a self-will that believes humans can solve anything that comes our way, and we have pushed God aside and view Him as irrelevant.

My purpose in writing *Leadership in a Lost Generation* is to challenge Christian leaders in every segment of society to lead like Jesus, based on the practical examples demonstrated through the life of Moses. God is a jealous God who will not be satisfied with our relationship with Him as a part-time experience. He wants to be involved in our lives on a daily basis and in a conscious way. He wants you to think about Him as your greatest asset along with the people you are leading. And why not? He is the source of truth and wisdom beyond any other that you could receive.

I am motivated to understand as much as I can about leadership. Are we born as leaders, or do we become leaders? I discovered that the answer is "both." We become leaders only when we discover something that we are truly passionate about and want others to join us. This is true as much in the business world as it is for a new mother who is passionate about giving her newborn the best that she can give because this new responsibility requires the functions attributed to "leadership."

Over the years, I have worked with a lot of people who are recognized as Christian leaders, whether they are business leaders, political and diplomatic leaders, church leaders, professionals in many fields, teachers, sports figures, or homemakers. One of the things that I observe is that contentment, for most, is short lived. The life of a person with considerable responsibility is filled with stress. How that stress is handled is really what this book is all about.

The effective management of stress can only be accomplished, with satisfaction, when we allow God into our lives to assist us with the challenges of life. Taking a break, consisting of a time away on a beach, at a cottage, or even on a cruise has its limits because wherever we go, we take the stress with us. So, as Christians, who do we need to take with us who is very capable of giving us a sense of peace? It is the Lord Himself. Why are so many missing the point?

The problem lies within our old nature that likes to control everything. We believe that control brings us security, so we engage our strengths, which are considerable, to solve every problem or opportunity that comes our way. We approach control in different ways depending on our personality, which I will discuss later. We are missing the point when we engage human strength before we ask the Lord to help us. Only when we get desperate do we seek the Lord for His input, and even then, we do so reluctantly. We are a proud people.

I love life, and I like to make a difference in peoples' lives. A love of life is given to me because of God's love. He loves me, and I love Him as my Father, as my Lord, and as my Teacher and Comforter. When I am obedient to Him, He gives me an amazing freedom to be the person He made me to be because I know that nothing stands in the way of my relationship with Him. I am forgiven! And this is the inspiration for delving into *Leadership in a Lost Generation.*

Barry Bowater

CHAPTER 1:

The Greatest of These Is ...

H AVE YOU EVER ASKED, "WHAT IS LEADERSHIP?" The answer to this question has been a lifelong passion of mine as I have sought to understand the essence of leadership through study and personal application, but mostly by watching others practice the principles through their use. My desire is to share this journey of understanding with you, and it begins with the influence of two couples, whom I will never forget, that taught me the most powerful principle of leadership that is the foundation to everything else that I have learned.

It was toward the end of summer 1984 when we arrived in our nation's capital, Ottawa, with expectations and fears that we could make a difference in the lives of political and diplomatic leaders.

This was the fifth move for our family in eleven years that had taken us across Canada twice and most recently from Toronto to Ottawa. There were now seven of us: Wendy and I, our four children, Christopher, twelve, Karen, ten, Joanne, seven, Peter, two, and Florence, Wendy's mom, who had lived with us since 1972.

We had been asked by the leadership of Campus Crusade for Christ, with whom we had served since 1973, to become the founding directors of a division called the Christian Embassy, a ministry to political and diplomatic leaders.

This was the fulfillment of a vision that the Lord had laid on my heart in 1978 as the result of a men's Bible study I was leading in Toronto. I encouraged them to reach out to their local political leadership to offer encouragement for their service and ask if they could pray for them. That challenge took me to Ottawa in 1978 to meet with my member of Parliament. Following a successful ninety-minute sharing time with the member and his daughter, I paused on the steps of the Confederation Building to reflect on the meeting. The Lord spoke to me about one day coming back to Ottawa and having a ministry for political and diplomatic leaders. Six years later, the call became a reality.

We settled into our new home in the Orleans suburb of Ottawa, registered three of our children in their new schools, and set off to Washington and New York for ministry training through the Christian Embassies that had been founded ten years earlier.

For more than two weeks, we experienced the highs and lows of attempting to minister to leaders in the US Congress and the diplomatic corps in Washington and New York at the United Nations. What we learned reinforced our vision that we were where the Lord wanted us to be in Ottawa, but we also realized that it would not be easy. We were about to discover the difficulties of establishing a ministry with people who were extremely busy, and meeting with us was seen as a low priority.

We arrived back in Ottawa in early October and set up an office on Laurier Avenue, about a ten-minute walk from Parliament Hill. There had been a general election in September, with a lot of change, and a new conservative government under the leadership of Prime Minister, the Right Honourable Brian Mulroney, who was elected with a sizeable majority. The change in government and all the activity surrounding the formation of a new cabinet, as well as newly elected members of Parliament (MPs) moving into new office space, made it very difficult to get appointments with anyone.

As a result, I focused on getting appointments with ambassadors or heads of mission in order to explain the purpose of the Christian Embassy and its value to the diplomatic community. I spent hours on the phone introducing myself to secretaries, "gate keepers," and administrative assistants, who were the ones I knew I must talk to in order to get appointments. For the most part, this was done without success.

During these early days of ministry, and out of frustration, I began to ask the Lord to open the doors to the people who could assist. Somehow, I had not made prayer a priority! The Lord answered by introducing Wendy and me to a couple who were well known in the diplomatic community, Roger and Mabelle Ladouceur. Roger had a prominent position in foreign affairs and Mabelle was in the travel industry and, as it turned out, dealt with many ambassadors on a personal level to arrange their travel needs. Most importantly, they had a passion to follow Jesus.

Several local people had offered to assist us in getting the Christian Embassy ministry up and running, but one person I had not called was Mabelle because I wondered how a travel agent would be helpful in this endeavour. Roger and Mabelle became wonderful friends, and we learned so much from each of them. They were the ones who taught us the rules of protocol on which Ottawa ran at the official level. As Roger insisted, if you want to meet and build a relationship with officials in the nation's capital, you have to do it by their rules.

I had no success in meeting with diplomats in the first month of ministry, but within the first week following a get-together with Mabelle, she and I visited with nine ambassadors to talk about the purpose of the Christian Embassy and why it was established. Mabelle simply called the ambassadors with whom she had a close business relationship and asked if we could pay them a visit.

These meetings were really the beginning of what would become an exciting ministry for Wendy and me, and many others, over the next seven years. The ministry is now in its fortieth year as a result of the relationships with the diplomatic corps, and with MPs. We were privileged to meet with government leaders around the world as the Lord opened the doors to foreign nations for the ministry in Ottawa to multiply. Our slogan became Christian Embassy Ottawa, "A Gateway to the World."

Of course, we ran into a few roadblocks along the way, not the least of which was the resistance by some of the diplomats opposed to the name "Christian Embassy." They explained, in a nice way, that Ottawa already had a Christian embassy in the form of the apostolic nunciature to Canada, or the official diplomatic representative of the Vatican in Rome. The ambassador is known as the apostolic nuncio (ambassador position) and at that time, he was the pro-nuncio, or most senior of diplomats, by order of tenure in Ottawa.

In other, not so nice ways, we were told that the nation's capital didn't need a nonofficial upstart organization that pretended to be an embassy interfering with official Ottawa. It fell on deaf ears that we were representing Jesus Christ and that we saw ourselves as His ambassadors as it says in 2 Corinthians 5:20, "Therefore, we are ambassadors for Christ, as though God were making an appeal through us; we beg you on behalf of Christ, be reconciled to God."

Once again, Roger and Mabelle provided a solution. Roger arranged for a luncheon for himself and I to meet with the pro-nuncio at his official residence in order for me to explain the spiritual purpose of the Christian Embassy. Roger was well known in diplomatic circles, as he was responsible for the ninth-floor hospitality section of the department of foreign affairs in those days. Today it is known as global affairs.

We had a wonderful lunch centred around a discussion on the role that Christ can play in the affairs of men and nations, with specific emphasis on the ministry of the Holy Spirit. The resistance within the diplomatic corps seemed to settle down after that luncheon, but it took the Canadian foreign affairs division a couple more years before they would offer briefings prior to our delegations to other countries that were initiated by diplomats posted in Ottawa and involved sitting MPs and Canadian business representatives.

For many more years, Roger and Mabelle continued to serve us in a variety of ways, including the time we arranged a delegation to Mexico, where Roger was posted as consul general. Our delegation included Col. Jim Irwin, Apollo 15 astronaut, who walked on the moon in August 1971, along with several MPs and business people. They put together a special dinner for distinguished guests, where Jim could share his moon landing experience and his faith in the Lord.

In November 1984, I was introduced to a number of parliamentarians who were willing to support the efforts of the Christian Embassy on "the Hill."

Girve Fretz was one, in particular, who became a very good friend, as he and his wife Lenore supported us in prayer and in making introductions to key people. Girve had been the mayor of Fort Erie, Ontario, just across the Niagara River from Buffalo, NY, and then ran for election as a member of Parliament in 1979, winning as a conservative member. In 1984, Girve played a strategic role in welcoming and supporting the new members of the conservative caucus, who were arriving to take their seats as elected members.

Girve played the same role with us. I remember meeting him for the first time in his office to explain the Christian Embassy ministry. Girve lived his faith, and he was truly excited to offer his support to our ministry. Following our meeting, he took me out in the hallway in West Block and shared with me his commitment to introducing me to as many of the members on that floor as possible. He also mentioned that there were two other Christian members in the same building, who would later play a significant role in the development of the Christian Embassy ministry, Len Gustafson and Ross Belsher. During the next several years, these members not only helped us to bring others to the dinners hosted by the Christian Embassy, but they would also travel with us on the delegations we took to Central America, five countries in Africa, and to Poland, Russia, and Ukraine between 1989 and 1990.

When I reflect on the role that Roger and Mabelle and Girve and Lenore played, among others, I am reminded that when the Lord calls us to do something, we are never left alone. Not only is He with us in the power of the Holy Spirit, but He has already placed key people in key positions to assist. Both couples had a genuine faith and trusted the Lord in life's circumstances. In addition, they were very sensitive to living a life of service to Jesus and, as a result, to their fellow humans. They served with joy and laughter in a world that is filled with demand and stress. They served the Lord with delight, and we were the beneficiaries.

Like most of the things that we attempt in life as Christians, a team of people is required to make a contribution, in one way or another, in order to produce the results. If there is one thing I have learned about leadership, it is that we cannot accomplish things on our own. I have often heard the statement that leadership can be lonely, and I would suggest if that were the case in your life, then I believe you are doing something wrong. You are trying to do things through your own resources, which ultimately leads to stress, and has the potential to impact your health and the way you deal with people.

Effective leadership requires a team that supports one another, encourages one another, has each other's backs through challenging circumstances, owns the results for what is being accomplished, and, especially, loves one another with Christ's agape love.

Wendy and I were blessed to work with a group of volunteers whom God provided and who demonstrated the characteristics found in 1 Corinthians 13, and they became the foundation of a successful ministry that continues to this day:

> If I could speak all the languages of earth and of angels, but didn't love others, I would only be a noisy gong or a clanging cymbal. If I had the gift of prophecy, and if I understood all of God's secret plans and possessed all knowledge, and if I had such faith that I could move mountains, but didn't love others, I would be nothing. If I gave everything I have to the poor and even sacrificed my body, I could boast about it, but if I didn't love others, I would have gained nothing.
>
> Love is patient and kind. Love is not jealous or boastful or proud or rude. It does not demand its own way. It is not irritable, and it keeps no record of being wronged. It does not rejoice about injustice but rejoices whenever the truth wins out. Love never gives up, never loses faith, is always hopeful, and endures through every circumstance.
>
> Prophecy and speaking in unknown languages and special knowledge will become useless. But love will last forever! Now our knowledge is partial and incomplete, and even the gift of prophecy reveals only part of the whole picture! But when the time of perfection comes, these partial things will become useless.
>
> When I was a child, I spoke and thought and reasoned as a child. But when I grew up, I put away childish things. Now we see things imperfectly, like puzzling reflections in a mirror, but then we will see everything with perfect clarity. All that I know now is partial and

incomplete, but then I will know everything completely, just as God now knows me completely.

Three things will last forever—faith, hope, and love—and the greatest of these is love *(New Living Translation)*.

Thank you to all the volunteers, politicians, and diplomats who serve with their hearts and helped to establish the Christian Embassy and its ministry to take the Gospel to leaders around the world.

CHAPTER 2:

Why Are We Lost?

WHY ARE WE LOST? THE SIMPLE ANSWER is because we don't know whom to trust as the source for truth.

An Ipsos survey taken in 2018 of nearly twenty thousand people aged eighteen to seventy-four living in twenty-three countries offered the following summary about whom we are able to trust.[1]

> While what is considered the most trustworthy profession varies by country, there is greater global consensus on professions considered to be untrustworthy.
>
> Politicians are considered the most untrustworthy profession in all of the countries surveyed–with two-thirds (67%) agreeing on this. Nearly six in ten people (57%) also said government ministers were not trusted–the second least trusted profession in fifteen countries.

There's also a divide over how much trust people have in those that are in authority and government versus professions in the private sector.

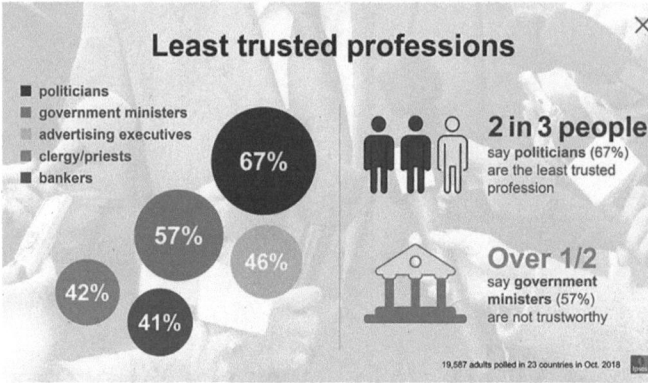

Least trusted professions

- politicians
- government ministers
- advertising executives
- clergy/priests
- bankers

67%
57%
46%
42%
41%

2 in 3 people
say politicians (67%) are the least trusted profession

Over 1/2
say **government ministers (57%)** are not trustworthy

19,587 adults polled in 23 countries in Oct. 2018

I would suspect that since this survey was taken more than five years ago, trust issues have increased in intensity. The Covid pandemic has resulted in more division between people than most have seen in a lifetime.

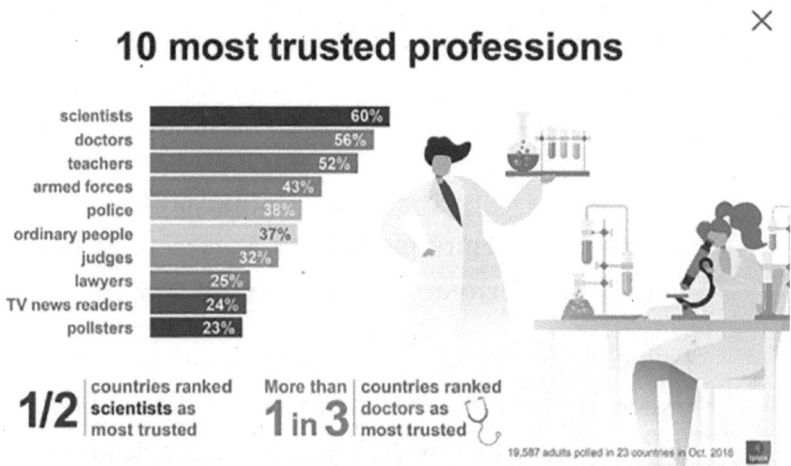

10 most trusted professions

Profession	%
scientists	60%
doctors	56%
teachers	52%
armed forces	43%
police	38%
ordinary people	37%
judges	32%
lawyers	25%
TV news readers	24%
pollsters	23%

1/2 countries ranked **scientists** as most trusted

More than 1 in 3 countries ranked **doctors** as most trusted

19,587 adults polled in 23 countries in Oct. 2018

Trust in science is devalued for many because the message has changed multiple times over the course of the pandemic due to the number of variables which forced change in the solutions offered to fight the disease. This, while people are told to trust the science. It is difficult to place your trust in something that is called "truth" if it is constantly changing. At least let us admit that "science" is a work in progress and not necessarily an absolute that we should live our lives by. Absolute truth doesn't change, and neither does God.

Politicians have been on the low end of the trust metre for a long time, and it has not improved with the increase in regulations that have limited the free movement of people. The media creates its own problem when it reports facts as truth based on their perceptions of truth, which is really their opinion, designed to influence the perceptions of others. What some call news can destroy confidence not only in the message, but also in the messenger.

Lack of trust in key institutions is one major reason why society is feeling lost. We don't know which way to turn in order to regain a sense of stability, and the result is that we turn inward in order to look after number one—ourselves—and those closest to us.

Leadership is based on trust, and trust is based on a set of values that instill trust in others. For example, I have been purchasing or leasing my vehicles from the same salesperson for nearly twenty-five years and the reason is that I trust him to give me a fair deal. His values express to me that he is working in my best interests and when that is true, I don't need to go anywhere else to purchase a car.

It is the same for companies for which I have consulted. When the emphasis is on customer "WOW," based on developing loyalty, and not just customer satisfaction or profits, the customers know that the organization they are doing business with will focus on meeting their best interests. The result is allegiance and repeat business for the company, dealer, or service supplier.

So, what are the values that develop trust? Allow me to explain using Diagram 2.1.

Diagram 2.1: The Influence of a Leader – A Person of Integrity

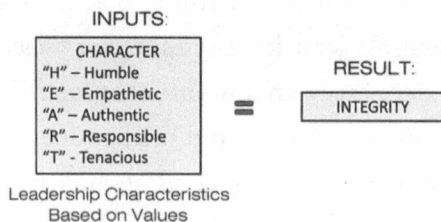

INPUTS:

CHARACTER
"H" – Humble
"E" – Empathetic
"A" – Authentic
"R" – Responsible
"T" - Tenacious

=

RESULT:

INTEGRITY

Leadership Characteristics
Based on Values

A measure of your character is defined by the values by which you live. Let's first look at the three relational characteristics, humility, empathy (compassion) and authenticity. These values reflect how you are able to relate to people.

Humility is the ability to serve others and to think more highly of others than you think of yourself. The ability to serve others requires love, patience, kindness, goodness, gentleness, and self-control.

Empathy is an understanding of what another person is going through. It's putting yourself in another person's shoes.

Compassion is a manifestation of empathy, and it is the ability to show kindness, caring, and a willingness to help others. Compassion and empathy are prerequisites for service.

Being **authentic** means that you are secure in yourself; you are satisfied with the way God made you, and you are not trying to become someone else. It takes a lot more energy to become someone else than it does to be happy with the person you are.

Being **responsible** and **tenacious** are the characteristics of purpose. Taking on responsibility and doing it well earns trust with people. Being tenacious means that you are doing things in a passionate way in order to produce a quality product or service.

The overall result of these foundational values is becoming known as a person of integrity–your walk matches your talk, and the results prove themselves.

To make this really effective in your life, you have to be able to trust yourself. This means that you have to know who you are from a personality perspective. Personality and character are different aspects of who you are as a person.

Your personality, and how you see yourself, has a lot to do with how you view the circumstances of life. If you are not happy with yourself, then you will have a tendency to be pessimistic or negative about events and people. If you are secure in yourself, that is you are happy with who you are as a person, then the opposite will be true. Attitude begins within, and it has a big impact on behaviour, and you are the one who controls your attitude.

I like the definition that Oswald Chambers uses to define personality. He says, "personality is the unique, limitless part of our life that makes us different from everyone else."[2] Chambers also says that we have difficulty measuring ourselves. I agree with this because the tools we use to try and measure our personality are finite. He goes on to say that only God really understands us, as He is the one who formed our personality in the first place!

In Jeremiah 1:5, the Lord says, "Before I formed you in the womb I knew you, before you were born, I set you apart."

We are all the same yet different! We are like fingerprints—at a distance they look the same, but under a microscope, they are unique.

This idea that God was very involved in our being is also found in Psalm 139:13, 15–16:

> For you created my inmost being, you knit me together
> in my mother's womb. My frame was not hidden from
> you when I was made in the secret place, when I was
> woven together in the depths of the earth. Your eyes
> saw my unformed body; all the days ordained for me
> were written in your book before one of them came
> to be.

A prerequisite for leadership is to understand yourself and how you behave. Let's begin by helping you, in a finite way, to understand your personality and the behaviours that go along with it. We have to know ourselves and the way God made us in order to understand the strengths and weaknesses of our personality.

Many of you have taken personality profile tests where you were asked to answer a series of questions and then at the end you were given a description of the "real" you. I have taken many of these over my career, and what I have discovered is that I don't change much in my basic profile.

I have been involved with the Adizes organization and its "change management" methodology for many years, both in an internal operational capacity with an organization I was engaged with in the 1990s, and for the last twelve years as an Adizes Associate working with faith-based, not-for-profit organizations as well as small - to midsize companies. Dr. Ichak Adizes is a master at understanding personalities, and he has developed a process for identifying them called the Management Style Indicator (MSI).

The MSI is based on the four roles of management that are required to run any organization, and these include managing your own life, the life of your family, your business or profession and, in many ways, the goals that you set for yourself and the planning process to achieve them. Diagram 2.2 defines these four roles.

Diagram 2.2: The 4 Roles of Management

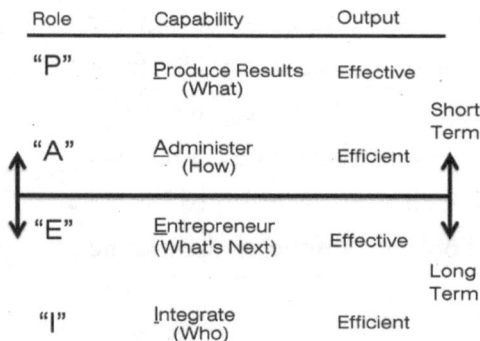

Role	Capability	Output	
"P"	Produce Results (What)	Effective	
"A"	Administer (How)	Efficient	Short Term
"E"	Entrepreneur (What's Next)	Effective	
"I"	Integrate (Who)	Efficient	Long Term

The **P role** of management is the ability to **produce** the results for which the organization was designed. It also stands for **purpose**, and answers the question "why does the organization exist?"

The **A role** is the **administrative** function for the organization, and its purpose is to provide efficiency in the short term.

The **E role** stands for **entrepreneur**, which is always asking the question "what's next?". This role is necessary for understanding changes that are essential to move ahead.

The **I role** stands for **integrator**, which focuses on the long-term development of people and their ability to work together. The integrator role is the key to success, as it keeps the organization focused on its vision and values and develops future leaders through the empowerment process.

The same four letters can also apply to people as a way of measuring **personality**. We are combinations of P, A, E, and I in varying degrees, and through a simple analysis, we can get a good idea of what our personality looks like. We will discover that we are good at some things and not so proficient at others.

I believe the influence that you can have on other people is shaped by a combination of your personality and your character as well as your vision and purpose in life.

Your personality is the default way of behaving, and as a result defines how you will tend to lead others. But we must remember that we are combinations of these four letters. Diagram 2.3 is an example of my Management Style Indicator (MSI), which reflects my personality.

Diagram 2.3: Personal Management Style Indicator

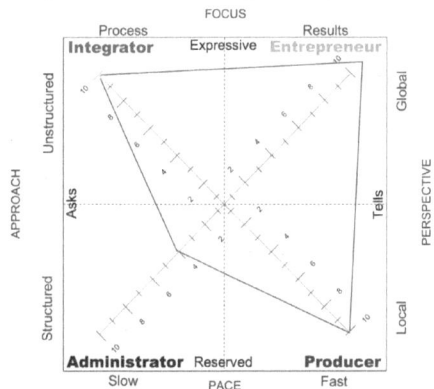

On the outside of the graph are the following descriptions:

Pace—the length of time it takes to decide something.

Approach—whether a person tends to be structured or unstructured.

Focus—defines the tendency to enjoy the journey (process) or if the person is rewarded by achieving results.

Perspective—determines viewpoint, which in simple terms is somewhere between boots on the ground (local) or a thirty-thousand-foot perspective (global).

People showing high results toward the top of the graph tend to be more **expressive** than those at the bottom, who tend to be more **reserved**.

People with high numbers on the right side of the graph tend to lean toward **telling** (speaking) people what to do, rather than the left side who prefer to **ask questions** (listen) for clarification before taking action.

I have attached my version of a survey and sample graph in the Appendix if you want to try this simple, non-scientific process for yourself. The statements in the survey are made up from my fifty-five years of experience watching how people tend to behave in a variety of situations, and reading Dr. Ichak Adizes' book, *Leading the Leaders.*[3]

Throughout the remainder of this book, I will be referring to management style by way of example to illustrate the significance of your personality in the way you behave. I will be emphasizing the two largest letters as defaults, and I am asking you to perform a self-analysis as you relate to the examples I will be sharing.

Let's take a closer look at the four basic management styles that I believe will help you to understand your personality and the need to develop character in order to provide a balance for your strong tendencies. The four style names below are attributed to Dr. Ichak Adizes.

The Lone Ranger Style: If you have a big P, Producer in your style, you will be very good at getting things done quickly. It won't take you long to figure out a plan unless you have a lot of A, Administrator, in your style as well. You are a hard worker, and your reward is getting things done. In fact, you will tell people to "leave it on my desk" and you will do it in time, depending on how many other things are piled on your desk as well. This is a problem for the big P because you can become a bottleneck as people have to wait for you to get to their priority issue. If you have a big P in your management style and you are leading people who are not meeting your expectations, you will tend to become very vocal in how you feel about their lack of performance.

The Bureaucrat Style: If you have a big A, Administrator in your style, you are a careful, linear thinker who will require more detail to decide. In one of my seminars, I asked a young woman with a big A how much detail she would need to decide. She answered quickly, "MORE!" It is possible for this style to have too much information for decisions because this style will have a problem prioritizing information. You tend to overthink everything, and it obviously slows down the process of getting things done. If you have a big A style and things are not going well in a meeting due to the lack of detail in the discussion, you will tend to keep your thoughts to yourself and internalize your frustrations to the point that you might stop communicating with people altogether.

A person with a big A is motivated to increase efficiency in any system, but they need to be careful that they do not try to achieve perfection. Because of change, perfection is very difficult to achieve. I also sense that big A's have a difficult time celebrating success because there is always something that is not quite right and needs to be fixed. Please remember, there is a fine line between efficiency and control.

I don't have a big A, Administrator in my style, but I have discovered, over the course of a lifetime, how valuable they are in creating efficiency within any organization by constantly asking "how" something should be done.

The Entrepreneurial Style: If you have a big E, Entrepreneur as part of your personality, you will be very creative in coming up with new ideas. As a warning to you, not every idea you have will be a good one because big E's have a tendency to disregard the "how" question. You will be visionary in your thinking, and you like to operate at the thirty-thousand-foot level as opposed to the P, Producer and the A, Administrator, who operate "boots on the ground." You love change, and you don't enjoy doing the same things over and over. You tend to be very impatient with people if they ask questions about your ideas or take too long in adapting them according to your expectations. Your reward, or satisfaction in life, comes through your ideas and creativity, but please be careful; you will tend to attack people who do not agree with you. Organizations and people will be limited in handling the constant changes that occur in life without the presence of the E style to offer input and direction.

The Integrator Style: The Integrator is a people person who loves to relate to others. They are people who can read the motive in others, as they have a strong ability to discern hidden messages. They don't say much within a group conversation because they are looking at body language nuances to "read" what is going on. If they have a high P, Producer, with the I, Integrator, they will quickly summarize what the group is saying and immediately provide a plan to move forward. High I style people without the P will resist conflict because they do not want to upset anyone, and as a result, when conflict occurs, they will have a difficult time deciding what to do next. The big I, Integrator, will be very sensitive to the other person's needs, and end up making excuses for poor performance because the big I will resist conflict like the plague.

The letter I stands for Integrator, a person who has a strong ability to bring people together in order to solve a problem or discuss an opportunity. The I, along with another large letter in their style, will be an effective leader, especially when the complementary team management approach is used to discuss issues, as in the family where parents must learn to become integrative leaders.

PI—A guide, leading and motivating a team to accomplish a task.

AI—A tactical leader, engaging a team based on logical input.

EI—A teacher, finding creative ways to get the best out of students.

We are seldom one dominant letter, and we must look at the traits of the other large letters in our style to get a clear picture of our natural tendencies.

Leadership is really about influencing others to follow, to contribute to a task, and eventually, multiplying your influence as a leader by adding value to others through their development of character and purpose. Diagram 2.4 illustrates the basic principles.

Diagram 2.4: Leadership is about influence and multiplication

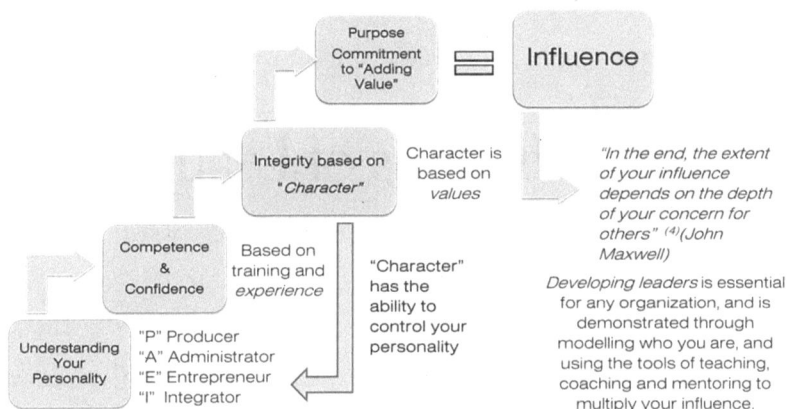

Every aspect of becoming an effective leader is based on trust and your ability to develop trust with others. Trust is based on truth, and for the Christian leader, your source of truth is found in your relationship with God, and it is the greatest asset you have in being able to influence others.

Let's examine the fundamental principles of our relationship with God and how they apply to becoming an effective leader.

CHAPTER 3:

The Foundations of Leadership

I HAVE ALWAYS ENJOYED WATCHING PEOPLE'S BEHAVIOUR, ESPECIALLY those who demonstrate leadership qualities and how they influence others. Many of the people I have observed never set out to become leaders, but that's where they ended up and people followed mainly

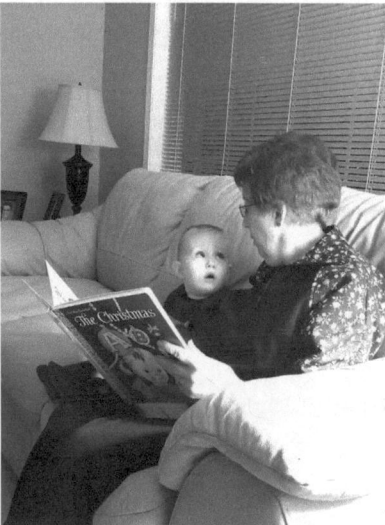

because they showed themselves to be trustworthy.

The relationship that my wife, Wendy, has with our grandkids is an example. They not only love her, but they also respect what she has to say, and no one more so than Connor, our youngest grandchild.

Many surveys have been done over the years asking the question, "Who has had the most influence on your life?" The common answer is, "My mother or grandmother." The basis of that relationship is found in trust and respect. Many mothers and grandmothers communicate a servant heart that reflects the best interest of the child or grandchild, and there is much that we can learn about leadership from them.

Leadership is not just about your personality or the development of your character, as important as they are. It is also important to define a personal purpose that will change through the course of your life depending on where you are on your personal journey and as you mature in your relationship with God.

I would like to take you on a journey with one of the most influential leaders in the Bible. Moses, a man who became a leader, lived for 120 years and learned to trust God. His legacy, written by his protégé Joshua, is referred to in Deuteronomy 34:10–12.

> Since then, no prophet has risen in Israel like Moses, whom the Lord knew face to face, who did all those miraculous signs and wonders the Lord sent him to do in Egypt—to Pharaoh and to all his officials and to his whole land. For no one has ever shown the mighty power or performed the awesome deeds that Moses did in the sight of all Israel.

More than two-thirds of his life can be described as "preparation" for the one-third that defined the impact of his leadership as described in the above passage. Being used by God is a lifelong journey for all of us, and every moment can be part of our growth curve if we remain open and teachable.

As a living document, the Bible is a practical leadership development resource because it contains the wisdom of God as it applies to humanity. When we study the lives of biblical leaders, we find they were confronted with every challenge that we have, and their initial default response was very much the same as ours would be if we faced the same tests, which, by the way, are common to all people.

As much as we are able to learn God's plan for humanity and His plan for the coming redeemer in the Old Testament, we also see the personal journeys of triumph and tragedy in those whom God used to write His revelation. Some scholars believe that Moses wrote the book of Genesis while he was living in the Midian desert. Moses didn't make it up; it was given to him by divine revelation. Moses also wrote the books of Exodus, Deuteronomy, and Numbers that define much of what took place during the Exodus of the Hebrew people and their forty-year journey to the Promised Land of Canaan. Moses also wrote the book of Leviticus, which defines the need for a deeper walk with the Lord, the need for obedience to God, and the laws upon which the relationship between humans and God was established prior to the revelation of the Messiah.

All of Moses's writings are worth reading for their historical accuracy and for the added blessing of understanding the character and purposes of God. I think of the book of Numbers as a daily journal of Moses's experiences as he provided the pastoral responsibilities of leadership for his people while at the same time dealing with leadership issues that every one of us will face at some point in our lives. The book of Deuteronomy was written toward the end of Moses's earthly life, and in many ways, it is a book of reflection. When we look back over the past forty years, we are bound to have a different perspective than we did forty years ago, and I believe this is demonstrated in Moses's writings.

Many biblical scholars believed that Moses was raised by his parents until the age of ten or twelve. He was born in Egypt at a time when the Hebrew people had lived in Egypt as refugees for just over three hundred years. They initially came from the east, from Canaan, during a time of famine, to be looked after by Joseph, the son of Jacob. Joseph grew up in a wealthy family that included eleven brothers. Scripture tells us that Jacob loved Joseph more than the others (Gen. 37:3). As a seventeen-year-old, he was quite boastful with his father and brothers, telling them that one day they would all serve him and be served by him. The brothers hated Joseph, and, unbeknownst to Jacob, the brothers sold Joseph to a caravan of Ishmaelites who were on their way to Egypt.

Through a long journey of personal growth, Joseph became a powerful ruler, second only to Pharaoh in the land of Egypt. Joseph, through God's wisdom, had overseen the Egyptian economy and the production of food to withstand the harshness of a coming seven-year drought that ultimately attracted Joseph's extended Hebrew family. The story of Joseph and his brothers can be found in the Bible in Genesis chapters 37–47, and it is a story of tragedy and triumph.

The Hebrew people settled in the land of Goshen, the most fertile part of the Nile delta, given to them by Pharaoh. Over the next three hundred years, and subsequent Pharaohs, the Hebrews increased in great numbers. They became a threat to the Egyptian leadership such that the pharaoh at the time of Moses's birth, thought to be around 1520 BC, had decreed that all male Hebrew babies were to be killed.

Hundreds of years before Moses was born, in Genesis 15:13–14, the Lord tells Abram the following:

> Then the Lord said to him, "Know for certain that for four hundred years your descendants will be strangers in a country not their own and that they will be enslaved and mistreated there. But I will punish the nation they serve as slaves, and afterward they will come out with great possessions.

Moses was born into a family of faith who believed God would deliver to them a very special child whom God would use to rescue the Hebrew people. I believe most parents believe their children are special, especially when they are babies, but this was different in the sense that they believed Moses was born to fulfill God's purposes. Moses's parents did everything they could to protect him from Pharaoh's edict by hiding him in the tall reeds growing in the shallow waters of the Nile.

As part of God's plan for Moses, he floated in a crude basket for three months, during which time he was hidden but cared for by his family. Guess who discovered him, and not by accident? Pharaoh's daughter found him and felt sorry for the little boy. Moses's sister was close by watching all this and asked Pharaoh's daughter if she should fetch one of the Hebrew women to nurse him. Guess who? Moses's mother was paid by Pharaoh's daughter to look after him. During the next ten years or so, Moses was trained in the traditions of the Hebrew people.

Exodus 2:10 tells us the next stage of God's plan for Moses:

> Later, when the boy was older, his mother brought him back to Pharaoh's daughter, who adopted him as her own son. The princess named him Moses, for she explained, "I lifted him out of the water" (*NLT*).

It is important for us to recognize the influences that have shaped us in our early years. For some it has been very loving and supportive, and for others, not so much. The early years shape our personality and the way we look at the circumstances of life, whether we see things from an optimistic or pessimistic perspective. The environment we grew up in has a big part to play in the development of our future thinking. Moses's faith traditions and the thought that God wanted to use him, influenced by his parents, caused him to doubt the significance of the training that he would receive in Egypt over the next thirty years, which motivated him to make life-changing decisions at the age of forty.

During the next phase of Moses's life, he was raised as the adopted son of Pharaoh's daughter, who did not have any sons of her own. This was a problem in Pharoah's Egypt, as the kingdom had to be passed on to a male heir. This next phase of Moses's life is described in the following passage: "Moses was educated in all the wisdom of the Egyptians and was powerful in speech and action" (Acts 7:22).

Moses was to receive training to become the next Pharaoh of Egypt, according to many biblical scholars, and as a result, he was taught to communicate effectively. Some believe he was trained to be a successful military leader in the most powerful nation in the world at that time.

Our training early in life does not always determine what we will end up doing as far as an occupation is concerned. Meaningful education teaches us how to think critically based on truth and personal values. In Moses's case, his personal values, taught by his parents, became the default over the values taught through his Egyptian training.

For many of us, our early training comes through practical experience, which has the potential to test our personality and our character. By the age of forty, Moses had become a man of action. The following passages in Exodus 2:11–15, tell us the following:

> One day, after Moses had grown up, he went out to where his own people were and watched them at their hard labor. He saw an Egyptian beating a Hebrew, one of his own people. Looking this way and that and seeing no one, he killed the Egyptian and hid him in the sand. The next day he went out and saw two Hebrews fighting. He asked the one in the wrong, "Why are you hitting your fellow Hebrew?" The man said, "Who made you ruler and judge over us? Are you thinking of killing me as you killed the Egyptian?" Then Moses was afraid and thought, "What I did must have become known."

> When Pharaoh heard of this, he tried to kill Moses, but Moses fled from Pharaoh and went to live in Midian, where he sat down by a well.

Moses was trained to take action. He was raised with a value system that told him he was special and that he would be used by God to free His people from slavery. He believed that his action of killing the Egyptian in defense of the Hebrews would result in the Hebrews following his leadership. The opposite happened!

Lesson number one for Christians in leadership is not to get ahead of God when He calls you do something.

In order for Moses to be able to fulfill God's expectations for leadership, he had to understand how to use God's strengths rather than his own. This is really a problem for all of us. Our personality dictates how we tend to operate, as I described in the last chapter, especially when we understand our default tendencies based on the two largest letters in our management style. In some ways, Moses had to go through a process of unlearning in order to understand what God had to teach him.

The result? Moses was forty years ahead of God. Genesis 15:13–14 states the prophesy given to Abram:

> Then the Lord said to him, "Know for certain that for four hundred years your descendants will be strangers in a country not their own and that they will be enslaved and mistreated there. But I will punish the nation they serve as slaves, and afterward they will come out with great possessions.

Moses's process of unlearning required teachability in order to understand what God had planned for his future. He was discouraged and fearful; he thought people would naturally follow him. He was now filled with self-doubt.

Leadership requires more than personality and skill. Moses had to understand God's leadership strategy based on a servant heart. That took forty years before God felt he was ready. It required God rebuilding Moses's self-worth and him learning to trust.

There is nothing like a personal crisis to get our attention. A crisis can defeat us or rejuvenate us. We can feel sorry for ourselves, or we can decide to learn from it and move forward. The next chapter in Moses's life was about moving forward, but it was only made possible through his dynamic relationship with God, and there is much we can learn from His abiding process.

CHAPTER 4:

Overcoming Barriers to Success

HAVE YOU EVER BEEN CHALLENGED TO DO something and almost immediately said "no?" It is far easier to say no to something than it is to say yes, especially if time and energy is required on our part. There are certain things that we have to evaluate in our lives when we are asked to do something difficult, particularly if we have faced disappointment or loss in the past. It takes some people longer to figure that out and regain a sense of confidence than others. For Moses, there was a lot to think about following his desire to help his Hebrew people, beginning with the question, "What went wrong?"

Regardless of the mistakes Moses made, God continued to provide for him through Jethro, the priest of Midian, who became his father-in-law and his family for the next forty years. Moses had plenty of time to reflect, and God used that time to reshape his thinking, his self-worth, and his future direction.

God first took care of Moses's physical needs by providing him with a job, a wife, and a family of his own. Secondly, God affirmed Moses's vision in a way that he would understand his purpose based on God's plan for the Hebrew people. There was nothing wrong with the vision that his parents had instilled in him during his early years of being God's choice to lead the Hebrew people out of slavery, but he needed to see where that fit within God's plan and the significance of God's timing for those events to take place.

During that forty-year desert experience, God did not abandon Moses, rather, He used the time to teach him the importance of timing and the division of responsibility between God Himself and Moses in leading the Exodus of the Hebrew people out of Egypt.

In like manner, we need to understand the role that we can play in helping to fulfill God's plan for our lives today. I believe God has a plan for all of us if we are willing to take the time to listen to what He is saying.

Wendy and I left the teaching profession in June 1973 because we felt a strong call to join a ministry whose goal it was to impact Canada with the Gospel of Jesus Christ, and, through Canada, have an impact on the world. We sold the first home we owned in Welland, Ontario, and moved more than three thousand kilometres west to British Columbia, and in some ways, really not knowing what exactly we would be doing. This move was not easy, especially as Wendy was eight months pregnant with our second child, and we had to raise our own salary and moving expenses from total strangers who supported the vision of our involvement in the ministry.

In the early days of this move, I really began to think that I had made a huge mistake. The security of the teaching profession and living in a nice home seemed far more attractive than what we were experiencing. Some of our friends thought we were crazy, even suggesting that we were outside of God's will. But God provided! We continued to receive encouragement from the leadership in the ministry that we had made the right decision because it fit with the vision that God had given to us.

As quick as Moses was to take action when he was forty years of age, his response to God at age eighty at the burning bush described in Exodus 3:1–6 was not nearly as responsive. But why?

For some, disappointment and defeat can take a lifetime to overcome because it is driven by an internal focus on ourselves. Some will seek the help of a professional in order to restore self-confidence, and the ultimate solution is to understand how to forgive yourself, understand your self-worth, and move on with life. The final stage in Moses's development as a leader was probably the hardest, and that was learning to accept who he was and to re-establish the confidence he had during his years in Egypt.

This is not about re-establishing confidence based on self-effort. As Christians, our confidence must be based on our relationship with God and His view of us. So, what does that mean?

1. God knew you before you were born.
   "For you created my inmost being;
   you knit me together in my mother's womb.
   I praise you because I am fearfully and wonderfully made;
   your works are wonderful,
   I know that full well" (Ps. 139:13–14).

2. God knows how long you will live, and He has a plan for you.
   "Your eyes saw my unformed body;
   all the days ordained for me were written in your book
   before one of them came to be" (Ps. 139:16).

3. God thinks about you all the time.
   "How precious to me are your thoughts, God! How vast is the sum of them!" (Ps. 139:17).

4. In God's eyes, you are unique, and you are loved by Him.
   "For God so loved the world that he gave his one and only Son,

that whoever believes in him shall not perish but have eternal life" (John 3:16).

If a relationship with God is based on Him forgiving us, what is stopping us from forgiving ourselves? The answer is unbelief—unbelief that God has the ability and power to forgive and that He wants to forgive you because He loves you. Some believe that their sin is too onerous to be forgiven. Others have told me that they will not allow anyone to forgive the things that they feel responsible for. His love is more powerful than pride, but often pride will close the door to accepting the love of another.

If you accept God's forgiveness, then you can begin to rebuild your confidence based on the confidence that God has in you as a unique creation of Himself, regardless of your age.

If you want to lead others or fulfill God's purpose for your life, then this is where you must begin. After being in the desert for forty years, Moses had the kind of relationship with God where he was not afraid to question God's affirmation of his calling to lead the Israelites out of Egypt through the burning bush experience in Exodus 3:5–15 and 4:1–17:

> "Do not come any closer," God said. "Take off your sandals, for the place where you are standing is holy ground." Then he said, "I am the God of your father, the God of Abraham, the God of Isaac and the God of Jacob." At this, Moses hid his face, because he was afraid to look at God.

> The Lord said, "I have indeed seen the misery of my people in Egypt. I have heard them crying out because of their slave drivers, and I am concerned about their suffering. So, I have come down to rescue them from the hand of the Egyptians and to bring them up out of that land into a good and spacious land, a land flowing with milk and honey—the home of the Canaanites,

Hittites, Amorites, Perizzites, Hivites and Jebusites. And now the cry of the Israelites has reached me, and I have seen the way the Egyptians are oppressing them. So now, go. I am sending you to Pharaoh to bring my people the Israelites out of Egypt."

God's timing for the Hebrew people to depart from Egypt was complete, and He believed Moses was ready to lead these people out of Egypt.

Moses knew this day would come. He had been thinking about it for many years, but he still had to overcome his self-doubt and his fear. Allow me to use quotes from John Maxwell from his daily devotional, *Leadership Promises for Every Day*.

> Brokenness involves removing inappropriate pride and self-reliance and building healthy God reliance. God tamed Moses's self-reliance and pride in the desert (forty years). To create trust, He had to break man's fears. Life is filled with trade-offs. Moses sacrificed his status and material possessions to prepare for his life of purpose. And then to fulfill it, he had to sacrifice again, relinquishing the security and safety of obscurity in the desert. To lead you must be ready to make sacrifices.[4]

God Deals with Moses's Fears

Moses shared with God his fears about being ready to take on such a heavy responsibility with four concerns, which God was ready to address.

1. Reaffirmation of his purpose.

Moses needed a reaffirmation of his purpose. He thought he was following God forty years earlier, and that resulted in failure.

But Moses said to God, "Who am I that I should go to Pharaoh and bring the Israelites out of Egypt?"

And God said, "I will be with you. And this will be the sign to you that it is I who have sent you: When you have brought the people out of Egypt, you will worship God on this mountain" (Ex. 3:11–12).

Moses is still thinking that what God was asking him to do depended on his personal skills. When God calls us to do something, it is through the relationship that we have with Him, and He supplies the wisdom, resources, and power to make it happen.

2. **Reaffirmation of who God is.**

Moses said to God, "Suppose I go to the Israelites and say to them, 'The God of your fathers has sent me to you,' and they ask me, 'What is his name?' Then what shall I tell them?"

God said to Moses, "I AM WHO I AM. This is what you are to say to the Israelites: 'I AM has sent me to you.'"

God also said to Moses, "Say to the Israelites, 'The Lord, the God of your fathers—the God of Abraham, the God of Isaac and the God of Jacob—has sent me to you.'

"This is my name forever, the name you shall call me from generation to generation" (Ex. 3:13–15).

3. **Reaffirmation of the authority question and the power of God.**

We all have asked this question at one time or another. Can I put my life in God's hands? Can I trust Him for the direction

He is taking me? Can He meet my needs and the needs of my family? Can I be fulfilled in what He is asking me to do?

The only alternative answers to this question are to trust yourself more than you trust God or trust the assurances of someone else who may be promising you the world.

Neither you nor anyone else can come anywhere near to providing what you need in order to equip you for God's service, and being in God's service should be the goal for every Christian regardless of occupation.

Moses was asking the same question that the Pharisees asked of Jesus hundreds of years later, and we are still asking today!

"Who gave you the authority to forgive people?" In addition, Moses wanted to be sure that people would recognize that it was God who sent him because of his rejection forty years earlier.

> Moses answered, "What if they do not believe me or listen to me and say, 'The Lord did not appear to you'?" Then the Lord said to him, "What is that in your hand?" "A staff," he replied. The Lord said, "Throw it on the ground." Moses threw it on the ground and it became a snake, and he ran from it. Then the Lord said to him, "Reach out your hand and take it by the tail." So, Moses reached out and took hold of the snake and it turned back into a staff in his hand. "This," said the Lord, "is so that they may believe that the Lord, the God of their fathers—the God of Abraham, the God of Isaac and the God of Jacob—has appeared to you."
>
> Then the Lord said, "Put your hand inside your cloak." So, Moses put his hand into his cloak, and when he took it out, the skin was leprous—it had become as white as snow. "Now put it back into your cloak," he

said. So, Moses put his hand back into his cloak, and when he took it out, it was restored, like the rest of his flesh.

Then the Lord said, "If they do not believe you or pay attention to the first sign, they may believe the second. But if they do not believe these two signs or listen to you, take some water from the Nile and pour it on the dry ground. The water you take from the river will become blood on the ground" (Ex. 4:1–13).

Moses was rejected forty years earlier by his own people, and for some, rejection is something that takes a lifetime to get over.

God was gracious in giving Moses a number of signs that would support his faith. Moses was cautious in his response to God as we would be if we have taken steps in the past to follow the Lord, and things appeared to go from bad to worse. These signs, and others, would be significant in convincing the Egyptian leadership that the God of the Hebrews was more powerful than any gods they had worshiped.

4. **Affirmation of confidence and courage.**

By this point in the discussion, Moses was getting desperate because he was running out of excuses. So, he chose to lie to God.

Moses said to the Lord, "Pardon your servant, Lord. I have never been eloquent, neither in the past nor since you have spoken to your servant. I am slow of speech and tongue" (Ex. 4:10).

In Acts 7:22 it says the following:

Moses was educated in all the wisdom of the Egyptians and was powerful in speech and action.

The Lord said to him, "Who gave human beings their mouths? Who makes them deaf or mute? Who gives them sight or makes them blind? Is it not I, the Lord? Now go; I will help you speak and will teach you what to say."

But Moses said, "Pardon your servant, Lord. Please send someone else" (Ex. 4:11–13, emphasis mine).

Have you ever felt like saying that?

Then the Lord's anger burned against Moses and he said, "What about your brother, Aaron the Levite? I know he can speak well. He is already on his way to meet you, and he will be glad to see you. You shall speak to him and put words in his mouth; I will help both of you speak and will teach you what to do. He will speak to the people for you, and it will be as if he were your mouth and as if you were God to him. But take this staff in your hand so you can perform the signs with it" (Ex. 4:14–18).

God responded to every concern that Moses had in order for him to overcome his doubts. Someone once told me that to overcome your fears, you have to live through them, and this would be true for Moses because the journey on which he was about to embark would provide every threat that Moses could imagine and beyond.

God does get frustrated with our lack of faith, but He remains faithful and gracious to us with our questions and doubts. God provided a partner for Moses—his own brother—to become his spokesperson and number two within the organizational structure for the Exodus to have success.

We are asking God the same questions, which are inspired by the battle that is going on within ourselves between our will and God's will. This is really a war between the pride of our old nature and God's will that is demonstrated through His Holy Spirit within us as believers.

Leadership is about trusting God in all circumstances. Those circumstances cannot be predetermined; so, we have to have a foundation of certainty within a life of uncertainty. Our relationship with God will provide us with that certainty, but it takes a lifetime journey with Him in order to understand as much as we can about the nature of that relationship.

Following six years of teaching high school students, and early in my career with Campus Crusade for Christ, I was given the opportunity to co-teach a management seminar to a large group of church leaders in Windsor, Ontario.

I felt comfortable because I would be co-teaching with a successful businessman and member of the US Campus Crusade Board of Directors from Eugene, Oregon. Clarence Brennerman had a neon sign business on the west coast and had practiced the principles of management in his business and in his church that we would be presenting at this three-day conference.

The closer we got to the date of the seminar; a nagging fear refused to leave me. I had been in the ministry less than a year, and I would be presenting to leaders who had been around a lot longer than me: I kept thinking to myself *"What happens if one of the pastors asks me about my credentials to teach this course—what do I say?"*

The first day went well, and the interaction and body language of the group was very positive—with one exception. A pastor sitting in the back row seemed rather surly and showed with every appearance that he didn't want to be there. I found out he was a pastor from a large church in Detroit, just across the river from Windsor. He would stay for a couple of sessions and then leave only to return several hours later. This bothered me, and I began to quietly ask the Lord what was going on with him. Well, he came back the second day and during one of the sessions he said, *"I have a question."* *"Yes sir,"* I responded. *"Why should I let an ex-school teacher and a sign painter (neon sign business) tell me how to run my church?"*

There it was; the very question I had feared for some time. I felt very comfortable presenting the material because it was logically laid out and we had adapted much of it in the church experience I had in Welland, Ontario, before we moved west. However, from a credential's perspective, my confidence was very low.

Did I really have the credibility to present this material? My mind raced with what to say, and I was now asking the Lord to please give me the words. Before I could open my mouth, one of the pastors stood up and faced the questioning pastor; *"Sir,"* he said, *"If you would care to attend all of the sessions, you would find that this material is the most useful information that you have ever received!"*

During the break, the pastor from Detroit left without a word and did not return. "Wow! Thank you, Lord, and thank you for using the pastor who responded to the question and who alleviated my fears."

Early on in our ministry, I learned that growth in confidence must be developed from within. It is not in my earned credentials or my experience, but my credibility must be founded in the relationship I have with the Lord and in the Holy Spirit who indwells me. A dependence on the Holy Spirit served us well throughout our ministry and it still does today because Jesus says, "I will never leave you or forsake you" (Hebrews 13:5).

There will be numerous times in our lives when our effectiveness for God is blocked by our pride as demonstrated in self-reliance and self-effort. We will also be stymied on occasion by our own fears in moving forward until we realize God's presence is within us.

In Hebrews 11:6 it says,

"And without faith it is impossible to please God, because anyone who comes to him must believe that he exists and that he rewards those who earnestly seek him."

In summary, our journey with God begins with God giving us life and the inspiration to make a difference in this world through our relationship with Him. This relationship is very personal, and it comes with God's resources to make a difference in our families, our occupations, and especially in ourselves. The barriers that Moses faced are the same ones that we face, and God is capable of overcoming them all—if we are willing to let Him do it.

CHAPTER 5:

Without Faith It Is Impossible to Please God

WHAT PICTURE DO YOU SEE IN YOUR mind when you think about God? Do you see a principled being based on His quality of character, or do you see a Heavenly Father who calls you His child? Oswald Chambers uses the example of Jonah in the Old Testament to share the difference between holding on to a principle about God and being obedient to acting on God's vision and purpose.

> There is a difference between holding on to a principle and having a vision. A principle does not come from moral inspiration, but a vision does. People who are totally consumed with idealistic principles rarely do anything. A person's own idea of God and His attributes may actually be used to justify and rationalize his deliberate neglect of his duty. Jonah tried to excuse his disobedience.[5]

Chambers goes on to describe the prophet Jonah's excuses not to do what God was asking him to do by using the principles of God's own character as an excuse in the Book of Jonah, "I knew that you are a gracious and compassionate God, slow to anger and abounding in love, a God who relents from sending calamity."

Jonah was called by God to go to Nineveh to share the following message in Jonah 1:1–3. "Go to the great city of Nineveh and preach against it, because its wickedness has come up before me."

Jonah responded by running away! "But Jonah ran away from the Lord and headed for Tarshish. He went down to Joppa, where he found a ship bound for that port. After paying the fare, he went aboard and sailed for Tarshish to flee from the Lord."

This didn't go well for Jonah, and you can read the rest of the story in the Book of Jonah. God's vision for Nineveh and Jonah's principle-based vision of God did not line up. Chambers goes on to say that we need to be careful to understand God's character <u>and</u> purpose as clearly as possible. It may be too easy for us to have a partial view of God based on His love for humankind but omit God's requirement for salvation such that His forgiveness is possible. It is our obedience to His offer of forgiveness that allows us to have the fullness of a relationship with Him.

Our vision of God must be more than a description of His character. We must know God for His heart, as that impacts everything we do. His heart has a passion for lost people, people who do not know Him personally, and a passion to use us to be part of His plan for the redemption of humankind.

God filled you with the Holy Spirit when you became born again, which means He gave you His character and the ability to become part of His vision and purpose. In other words, He gave you the resources to do His will here on earth.

I encourage you to evaluate not only your relationship with God, but also the depths of what you believe about Him. For some, it is tempting to accept the things that you like about His character and ignore the fact that He holds us accountable for our actions based on what He considers to be right and wrong.

The leadership development journey never ends while we are here on this earth, but it must be built on trust in God and fed with the fires of God's passion. Whether your leadership focuses on your family, your business, your profession, or the people you meet along the way, you must continue to ask these questions: "Am I expecting God to do greater things than He has ever done before? Is there a freshness and a vitality in my spiritual outlook?"

In the early days of the Exodus, Moses's journey of leadership development took him through several life-changing experiences that became a foundation of understanding for his remaining forty years of life.

The first one took place within a few weeks of getting started on their journey to the Promised Land, and it came when they arrived at the crossing of the Red Sea (Gulf of Aqaba) in order to cross to the land of Midian.

In the early 1990s, I travelled extensively with Col. Jim Irwin, Apollo 15 astronaut who walked on the moon in the 1971 mission with David R. Scott, Commander, James B. Irwin, Lunar Module Pilot, and Alfred M. Worden, Command Module Pilot.

Jim was a very committed Christian and explorer, not only in outer space, but also here on earth, searching for evidence of biblical history. I heard many stories while we travelled in Central America, Mexico, Poland, Russia, and Ukraine, and as he came to Ottawa to be a guest speaker at our Christian Embassy dinners for politicians and diplomats.

During one of his early exploits, following his career with NASA, he nearly lost his life in Turkey when he fell down the side of a mountain while searching for evidence of Noah's Ark.

On another adventure, Jim led an exploration with a few biblical researchers to try to find proof of the Exodus, taking deep dives into the Gulf of Aqaba to discover preserved evidence of chariot parts that would have been submerged for more than three thousand years. He also took a clandestine journey into western Saudi Arabia, attempting to locate what he believed to be Mt. Sinai. There, he saw a mountain with the top third blackened as with severe heat and, in the valley below, a site that contained evidence of gold deposits as measured with a metal detector.

In 1992, I was privileged to accompany Canada's minister of energy, mines, and resources on a trip to the Middle East following the first Gulf war. We left Riyad, Saudi Arabia, and flew north along the eastern shore of the Red Sea heading to Cairo, Egypt. I was able to take several pictures from the plane looking east toward what was known in biblical times as the Land of Midian.[6]

The map below is referred to in Exodus 14:1–2, "Then the Lord said to Moses, tell the Israelites to turn back and encamp near Pi Hahiroth, between Migdol and the sea. They are to encamp by the sea, directly opposite Baal Zephon."

Jim believed that the location of God speaking and dictating the Ten Commandments to Moses on the mountain, which many have labeled as Mt. Sinai, was in the land of Midian (presently Saudi Arabia), as the map illustrates.

Before the journey to cross the Red Sea (Gulf of Aqaba), Moses was to face one of the toughest tests of leadership he would confront.

The Israelite people were on their way to the Promised Land by way of the Sinai Peninsula that took them to the northern shore of the Gulf of Aqaba. As instructed by God, they were to camp there at a place called Pi Hahiroth (Ex. 14:2). This journey was not the direct route to the land of Canaan, which was a common trade route in those days for caravans to travel the two-week journey between Egypt and Canaan.

God was leading the people through the presence of His angel, who provided direction via a cloud by day and a pillar of fire by night. He had His reasons for the indirect route. Many Israelites had adopted Egyptian traditions and idols and there was little evidence of a close relationship with the Living God. The indirect route would give them time to get organized and to be educated in the Abrahamic traditions. Early in the journey they would receive God's laws for the well-being of their life and faith. God spoke to them through their leader, Moses. The place of encampment would provide a major lesson in the fact that their God, who had rescued them from Egypt, could be counted on for their daily security as well.

Pharaoh set out to pursue the Israelites, believing them to be totally lost and easily defeated. The Israelites saw them coming with their six hundred chariots and troops, creating a dust cloud that could be seen from miles away. Their response was quite normal for people who fear for their lives:

> As Pharaoh approached, the Israelites looked up, and there were the Egyptians, marching after them. They were terrified and cried out to the Lord. They said to Moses, "Was it because there were no graves in Egypt

that you brought us to the desert to die? What have you done to us by bringing us out of Egypt? Didn't we say to you in Egypt, 'Leave us alone; let us serve the Egyptians'? It would have been better for us to serve the Egyptians than to die in the desert!" (Ex. 14:10–12).

Moses had been rejected by these people once, forty years earlier, and now they were blaming his leadership once again, but this time he had a different response.

Moses answered the people, "Do not be afraid. Stand firm and you will see the deliverance the Lord will bring you today. The Egyptians you see today you will never see again. The Lord will fight for you; you need only to be still" (v. 13).

This was a bold statement based on his growing faith and the promises that God had given to him prior to the journey.

The next verse is interesting to me as it appears that an additional conversation between Moses and God is missing. The Lord spoke to Moses right after Moses's statement above.

Then the Lord said to Moses, "Why are you crying out to me? Tell the Israelites to move on. Raise your staff and stretch out your hand over the sea to divide the water so that the Israelites can go through the sea on dry ground."

There are many times on our leadership journey when we speak with boldness and then second-guess ourselves and hope that God will show up to make happen what we cannot do alone! God did provide a miracle by parting the waters that allowed the Israelites to escape the Egyptians and continue the journey into the land of Midian. This is the same God in whom we can trust today.

The journey that started in Egypt would not be a simple one that would last for two weeks. There were upwards of three million people travelling the Exodus route that today, which we would consider a logistical nightmare! God gave them an opportunity to enter the Promised Land two years after they began but they refused, so the journey lasted forty years before they were ready to cross the Jordan River. God met their physical needs every step of the way, but it took thirty-eight years longer than necessary because they refused to learn the spiritual lessons of trusting God rather than depending on their own human nature, which is often motivated by fear and pride.

There is not much difference with the world that we are living in today. Leading people is a challenge, and we will be tested in all kinds of circumstances and differences of opinion based on a different set of values than the ones we live by as Christians. When God calls us to lead, He supplies the resources to get the job done, whether that is the process of what needs to happen in order to reach the goals you are trying to achieve or dealing with the people for whom you are responsible. There are many lessons from the forty-year journey that Moses took in the desert that we can learn from, and I would like to share some of the things that I have appreciated from studying his life as a leader.

In the next chapter, we will look at how God gave Moses the resources to deal with the issue of rebellion.

CHAPTER 6:

The Toughest Part Is the People

Several years ago, I attended a small management training seminar in California with eight or nine people, including the young but experienced presenter. One of the attendees was a businessperson who was originally from Israel, now living in California.

It was not long into the first session that the businessperson interrupted to offer his perspective on the presentation. The presenter responded in a thoughtful way and then continued. Not long afterward, the businessperson interrupted again, this time in a more forceful manner. Again, the presenter responded graciously. This behaviour continued throughout the morning session, with most of us getting frustrated with the ongoing intrusions. Finally, the presenter made a point of saying that most of the people who came to the seminar wanted to benefit from the content and not to listen to someone who had an opinion based on what he felt was a better idea.

I have often thought about this experience What I have discovered is this form of exchange is very cultural. Israel's national culture is based on the entrepreneurial style of management. This is a visionary, creative, risk-taking culture that is often asking, "What's next?" The entrepreneur is always thinking about a better way to do something, and this businessperson was an entrepreneur. It was normal for him to argue based on thinking that what was being presented could be improved. As God's chosen people of the Old Testament, it is not surprising that Moses's leadership over the next forty years would be faced with challenges from a people who were averse to following anyone, believing that there was always a better way to do something.

Rebellion is a foundational characteristic of our human nature. It is driven by pride and manifested in a variety of ways, only one of which is outward expression.

It really depends on your default personality. Ask yourself, "How do I express disagreement—verbally or nonverbally?" If you have a big A, Administrative style, you will tend to be nonverbal in your disagreements. This happens in meetings where big P, Producers, and big E, Entrepreneurs, dominate the meeting with their ideas and their desire for quick results without much thought for how something should be done. The Administrative type gets very frustrated with this approach, but they will seldom say anything. They are sitting down on the outside, while standing up on the inside!

Likewise, the big I, Integrator, will not say much because they avoid conflict. Their idea of a good meeting is when unity occurs; but this unity is a false measurement if every style has not been given the opportunity to express their thoughts. Big P's tend to ignore silence and dominate the conversation with their ideas while big E's view silence as agreement, especially when they are sharing their ideas.

Moses would face it all during his forty years of leadership, and it would be a test of his relationship with the Lord and with the people who would be closest to him. Here is the first challenge that I will share in the next several chapters to illustrate the issues involved and how Moses dealt with them, which I trust will be helpful in your leadership experiences.

The Golden Calf

Shortly after arriving in the land of Midian, Moses was called up to meet with the Lord on the mountaintop high above where the Israelites were camped. Aaron was left in charge. God would share His moral law, the Ten Commandments, and the principles for successful living with Moses, for forty days. These instructions are found in Exodus chapters 19 - 32.

Pride can be manifest in selfishness, and the Israelites were not immune to expressing their displeasure when things didn't go their way. For example, in Exodus 17:2, they complained because there was a lack of water, so, "They quarreled with Moses and said, 'Give us water to drink.'" Moses's response was appropriate. "Why do you quarrel with me? Why do you put the Lord to the test?"

Your leadership will be tested continually throughout your career, and your relationship with the Lord must allow you the freedom to cast your burdens on Him as expressed in Matthew 11:28–30:

> Come to me, all you who are weary and burdened, and
> I will give you rest. Take my yoke upon you and learn
> from me, for I am gentle and humble in heart, and you
> will find rest for your souls. For my yoke is easy and
> my burden is light.

After forty days, the people were tired of waiting for Moses to come down from the mountain, even though they had heard the voice of the Lord previously as described in Exodus 19, as well as having seen the demonstration of God's power through fire and smoke at the top of the mountain. On that earlier occasion, the elders of the people responded with obedience in Exodus 19:8, "We will do everything the Lord has said."

The Exodus was three months into the journey, their faith was based on what they could see and experience, and their leader was taking far too long in his absence. They had approached Aaron with the following request, found in Exodus 32:1–5:

> When the people saw that Moses was so long in coming down from the mountain, they gathered around Aaron and said, "Come, make us gods who will go before us. As for this fellow Moses who brought us up out of Egypt, we don't know what has happened to him."
>
> Aaron answered them, "Take off the gold earrings that your wives, your sons and your daughters are wearing, and bring them to me." So, all the people took off their earrings and brought them to Aaron. He took what they handed him and made it into an idol cast in the shape of a calf, fashioning it with a tool. Then they said, "These are your gods, Israel, who brought you up out of Egypt."
>
> When Aaron saw this, he built an altar in front of the calf and announced, "Tomorrow there will be a festival to the Lord." So, the next day the people rose early and sacrificed burnt offerings and presented fellowship offerings. Afterward they sat down to eat and drink and got up to indulge in revelry.

There are several observations that I would like to make from this passage that I believe we are dealing with today.

1. The level of faith among people, even many Christians, is limited and very much influenced by fear.

2. Most people will respond to authority because they believe that their security is found in the "system." Aaron represented the

authority because Moses had left him in charge. Authority is a powerful tool in leadership, but we need to be very careful about how we use it. In the Adizes methodology, authority is defined as the legal right and obligation to say, "yes" *and* "no." In Aaron's case, he did not use his authority effectively in being able to serve God's interest and purpose for the Exodus (see point 4).

3. Many people in leadership today will express a trust in God, but their level of trust is not necessarily deep and personal.

4. Leaders are motivated by the need at hand, and their personality will dictate how they will respond. In the case of Aaron, I believe he was afraid of the people and basically figured out a way to appease them. Leaders must be cautious about moving people into positions of authority too quickly unless their level of authority has been tested. Leadership must have a base of stability found in a set of values that provides evidence of integrity.

5. The way people celebrate is often an indication of their level of maturity and self-discipline. Getting drunk demonstrates a lack of self-control.

God shared with Moses what was happening in the Israeli camp where Aaron had allowed the people to get out of control.

> "Go down, because your people, whom you brought up out of Egypt, have become corrupt. They have been quick to turn away from what I commanded them and have made themselves an idol cast in the shape of a calf. They have bowed down to it and sacrificed to it and have said, 'These are your gods, Israel, who brought you up out of Egypt.' I have seen these people," the Lord said to Moses, "and they are a stiff-necked people. Now leave me alone so that my anger may burn against them

and that I may destroy them. **Then I will make you into a great nation"** (Ex. 32:7–10, emphasis mine).

So how did Moses respond? He demonstrated his commitment to serve the very people he was leading and pleaded with God to reconsider His judgement, even though God was prepared to destroy these people and start over again through Moses himself.

When you are in a leadership position, there will be times that you will be very frustrated with the people you are leading. You are giving your best, and some are not responding. Be careful that you do not act based on your emotions. Take time to settle down, breathe deeply, and ask the Lord how you should respond. From my experience, He will tell you what to do. Here is Moses's response:

> But Moses sought the favor of the Lord his God. "Lord," he said, "why should your anger burn against your people, whom you brought out of Egypt with great power and a mighty hand? Why should the Egyptians say, 'It was with evil intent that he brought them out, to kill them in the mountains and to wipe them off the face of the earth'? Turn from your fierce anger; relent and do not bring disaster on your people. Remember your servants Abraham, Isaac and Israel, to whom you swore by your own self: 'I will make your descendants as numerous as the stars in the sky and I will give your descendants all this land I promised them, and it will be their inheritance forever.'" Then the Lord relented and did not bring on his people the disaster he had threatened (Ex. 32:11–14).

Moses interceded with God based on God's own character and His promises.

1. He reminded God that these people were His people and they did not belong to Moses. Moses was simply the leader that God chose to lead the Exodus.

2. Non-Christians will question our character and the character of God. When a major disaster happens, how many times do we hear, "Why would God allow this to *happen?*". People are often quick to blame God, especially when they don't have a close relationship with Him. God is true to His promises, evidenced by the rescue of His people after they had lived in Egypt for four hundred years.

3. God is the same yesterday, today, and forever, and He will not, and cannot go back, on the promises that He made to Abram and the one He makes to us: that He will never leave us or forsake us.

Moses then had to go from the mountain and deal with the rebellion that Aaron had let get out of hand. There are consequences that we need to deal with in leadership, and sometimes it means letting people go from our organization. A spirit of rebellion will always have consequences on the culture of the organization unless you are prepared to deal with it. "And the Lord struck the people with a plague because of what they did with the calf Aaron had made" (Ex. 32:35).

Some would consider Moses's actions as his greatest moment. He was committed to serving his people, which motivated him to intercede for them whenever they got themselves into trouble. God would call them a stubborn, stiff-necked people, and this is true of some of the people we will meet along life's journey. One thing we can do for people that behave this way is to intercede for them in prayer and trust the Lord that He will change their hearts and their attitudes.

CHAPTER 7:

Serving Others–
The Foundation of Leadership

I WAS NEVER REALLY MOTIVATED IN MY YOUTH by the thought of serving others. I have always been a "doer." I love to get things done, and completing a project was always a reward for me.

That sounds selfish, but I was always motivated by the P, Producer, role of management more than anything else. That is until I discovered the I, Integrator role of management in my experiences as a team leader in Sea Scouts as a young man. There was nothing I enjoyed more than taking a group of young men away for a

sailing weekend up the Ottawa River in our troop's navy whaler and teaching the art of seamanship as I was taught a few years earlier.

Today, I am motivated by getting things done through individuals and teams of people, and, in the process, helping to develop them in their roles. This is the PI role of leadership, which is defined as a Guide.

How do we learn the essentials of serving others, and how do we benefit from the results of serving others within our leadership function? I believe there are two things that we can learn from Moses's journey that allowed him to lead two to three million people in the Exodus. One is growth in our character, and the other is the significance of structure as a means to communicate vision and purpose and to delegate responsibility.

The Spiritual Foundation of Service—Growing in Character

Human nature is a powerful force within each of us and our default tendency is to look after ourselves first. So, how do we get to the point of not only wanting to serve others, but doing something about it? It begins with an understanding of what happened to you when you became a born-again Christian. The Holy Spirit entered your life to begin the journey of living according to a new nature, Christ's nature. As it says in 2 Corinthians 5:17, "Therefore, if anyone is in Christ, the new creation has come: The old has gone, the new is here!"

We will all discover that living according to a new nature is really a work in progress. In 1 Peter 1:13–16, the apostle is sharing his insights as to what that looks like (emphasis mine):

> So, **prepare your minds for action and exercise self-control.** Put all your hope in the gracious salvation that will come to you when Jesus Christ is revealed to the world. So, you must live as God's obedient children. Don't slip back into your old ways of living to satisfy your own desires. You didn't know any better then. **But now you must be holy in everything you do**, just

as God who chose you is holy. For the Scriptures say, "You must be holy because I am holy."

This defines the battle that we are dealing with in our lives as Christians—the battle between the old nature that we are born with, and the new nature when we are born again. We must always keep this perspective in focus: "prepare your minds for action and exercise self-control." If we try to live according to the new nature with the abilities of the old nature, we are in for a tough go and will become very frustrated. This leads to legalism, which is a constraint on our spiritual life. So, we must live according to the power of the new nature within us through the presence of the Holy Spirit and the freedom that forgiveness grants us.

We have an obligation to God when we are born again and receive His forgiveness, as it says in 1 Corinthians 6:19–20:

> Do you not know that your bodies are temples of the Holy Spirit, who is in you, whom you have received from God? You are not your own; you were bought at a price. Therefore, honor God with your bodies.

The price Jesus paid for us was His own death on the cross at Calvary. He died to set us free from slavery to our deadly old nature as it says in Romans 8:1–2 and 5–10:

> Therefore, there is now no condemnation for those who are in Christ Jesus, because through Christ Jesus the law of the Spirit who gives life has set you free from the law of sin and death. ... Those who live according to the flesh have their minds set on what the flesh desires; but those who live in accordance with the Spirit have their minds set on what the Spirit desires. The mind governed by the flesh is death, but the mind governed by the Spirit is life and peace. The mind governed by

the flesh is hostile to God; it does not submit to God's law, nor can it do so. Those who are in the realm of the flesh cannot please God. You, however, are not in the realm of the flesh but are in the realm of the Spirit, if indeed the Spirit of God lives in you. And if anyone does not have the Spirit of Christ, they do not belong to Christ. But if Christ is in you, then even though your body is subject to death because of sin, the Spirit gives life because of righteousness.

The more you walk with God and trust Him with every aspect of your life, the more you will recognize that He will share His character with you as you abide in Him. The measure of our growing maturity in Christ is the growth of our character. Our character takes on Christ's character, which is the source of our ability to serve others. We do not naturally desire to serve others, but we do so when the character of Jesus motivates us and we are obedient to His instruction. The added benefit of taking on the character of Christ is experiencing the ability to control our personality.

We have access not only to His character, but also to His mind and Spirit. 1 Corinthians 2:15–18 says (emphasis mine):

> The person with the Spirit makes judgments about all things, but such a person is not subject to merely human judgments, for, who has known the mind of the Lord so as to instruct him? **But we have the mind of Christ** (also reference Isaiah: 40:13).

We have access to the mind of Christ, and He provides us with truth, wisdom, discernment, intuition, and insight when we are working with and serving others.

To effectively serve others in leadership, we must decide that we are willing to share the credit with others whenever good things happen, while at the same time, we must be willing to take responsibility when things don't quite work out according to plan. This is not easy because our egos, our old nature, are involved. If you have a high producer mentality and people are not moving quickly enough, you will tend to want to take over. The key to developing others is allowing them to learn in the doing.

You can't develop people in a vacuum; you must let them take steps of faith. In the early days, your role in serving them is to help manage the failures and keep people encouraged and moving forward.

I loved playing hockey, and I coached my son's Pee Wee hockey team. Helping to coach young players on a sports team is a good way to learn the process, mainly because it teaches patience. When things don't go as planned with a young team of players, one of the things that you cannot do is put on your equipment, get on the ice, and help them out. First, it would look ridiculous, and second, that is not your role. My job as a coach was to input the basics in terms of skill, team play, and motivation. There were times during our team's playoff runs where we would go into overtime with the game tied and kids would come to the bench to try to get off the ice for a replacement. "Why?" I would ask, knowing that they just got out there. "I don't want to be on the ice if we get scored on," they replied. I responded, "I need you on the ice, son; we want to score first!" Letting go and letting others perform without fear is something that I learned in my coaching experiences.

This is no different when working with adults in any organization if you are a team leader. You must perform your role and leave the results to the talent that was hired to do the job or to the ones who volunteered. In fact, you have three functions as a team leader: you are a **teacher**, sharing the basics of how you want the team to accomplish the task, you are a **coach**, showing individuals how to do something, and you are a **mentor**, dealing with the personal and emotional side of human nature when people are working together.

If you are privileged to lead a team, I trust you notice the responsibilities you have in serving others. You are developing individuals to perform well while at the same time encouraging them to adapt to the culture in which you want the team to engage. These principles are true for raising a family as well.

You are also developing a team approach to accomplishing a task in a complementary fashion that allows the team to achieve the results they are aiming for. Your role is to put the right people in the right roles, which initially is a process of trial and error. You will not be able to really understand people until you see them in action. Personality profiles will only tell you so much, mainly a person's default tendencies. They will not tell you much about character until you see them in action, especially in the areas of taking responsibility, dealing with people, and their passion for the job.

In addition, you are the one who must develop the culture of the team that focuses on mutual trust and respect between each member of the group. They must respect each other's differences and trust that they will have each other's backs in producing the overall team results. Finally, as a team leader and developer of people, you are also responsible for the results.

Serving others requires trust and respect. In any relationship, especially in teaching, coaching, and mentoring, trust must be established for the input to be effective. Teaching is often less personal, but it still requires trust and respect, and it is foundational for understanding the principles of something or reminding people why they are doing what they are doing. Once the trust factor is established with an individual or a team, your role as a leader is to empower people to do their job with confidence and to develop their sense of ownership, meaning doing the job well in the best interests of the organization.

How do you build confidence among people who are starting a new job or finding themselves in a new environment? Team success is a great way to do it, and as team leader you must create some early wins. Even if the results of working together are not great, you will still have some key learning points that you can talk about. There is safety in numbers. No one person must take the full responsibility for the results. The responsibility must be a team responsibility—we win together, or we do better together next time.

It takes a lot of energy to develop people, and when we are working with Christians, we are sharing with them spiritual principles and leadership principles at the same time. You must be committed to the people you are developing, and you must use all of your relational skill, wisdom, and discernment from the Holy Spirit to understand how to motivate and develop different personalities.

Diagram 7.1 illustrates your role and responsibility in leading others. The most significant role of leadership in team building is the "I" role, or Integrator role.

Please note the image of the hand, especially the function of the thumb. The thumb is the only digit on the hand that is effective in working with the other four digits. It is the only digit that can close the gap with another digit to be able to hold something with strength. This is the illustration that Dr. Adizes uses to demonstrate what leadership is all about.[7] The digits represent the team members, and the thumb represents the leader. Together they form a complementary team to fulfill the team goals.

Diagram 7.1: Your Role as a Leader is to Create a Safe Place for the Team

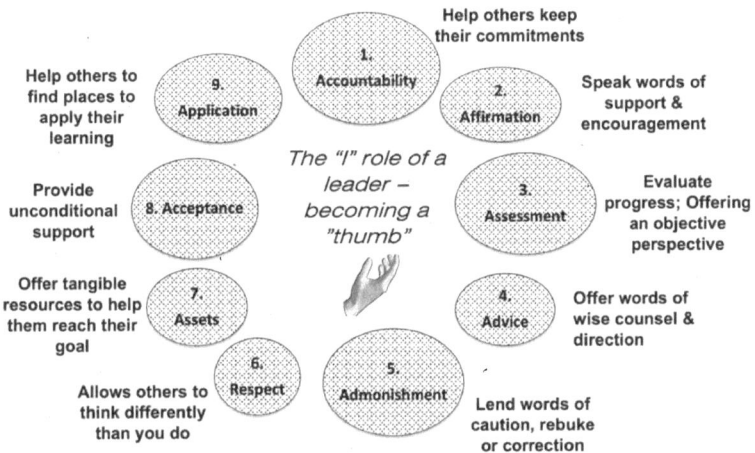

Help others keep their commitments

1. Accountability

Help others to find places to apply their learning — 9. Application

Speak words of support & encouragement — 2. Affirmation

The "I" role of a leader – becoming a "thumb"

Provide unconditional support — 8. Acceptance

Evaluate progress; Offering an objective perspective — 3. Assessment

Offer tangible resources to help them reach their goal — 7. Assets

Offer words of wise counsel & direction — 4. Advice

Allows others to think differently than you do — 6. Respect

5. Admonishment

Lend words of caution, rebuke or correction

What does a powerful team look like? From a functional perspective, the four roles of management that I spoke about in Chapter Two are institutionalized within the team. The team represents all four roles, not just the roles that are their strong points. Powerful teams are dependable because they operate with a positive motive that considers the best interests of the organization. They are responsible for making decisions through the process of sound thinking that take into account all the variables. They are visionary in their approach to new ideas and strategies. They are consistent in their contribution to be accountable to one another and tenacious in making things happen.

In the language of Adizes, the thumb is the symbol of leadership, the Integrator role, that has the ability to develop the team toward a common purpose and with a common sense of ownership.

This represents the modern form of management that is replacing the top-down management model. When the I, Integrator role is functioning well, all members of the team will have input into the process, while also having responsibility and ownership for the results.

It is this role that focuses on people and their development. I have discovered that a person's I role can grow with the development of character. The P, Producer, A, Administrator, and E, Entrepreneur roles don't seem to change much in most of the people that I have evaluated, including myself. What does change is the maturing of positive values, which can have a strong influence on the growth of the I, Integrator, style within your personality.

It is this role that maintains a consistent, positive culture. And it is this role that emphasizes shared purpose, values, and mission all within a culture of mutual trust and respect, with an emphasis on sustained leadership development for the future.

As Christians, we are instructed to make disciples. Leadership is the ability to influence others to fulfill a purpose. Disciple-making requires us to be leaders because we are influencing people to consider the value proposition that God is offering through a relationship with Jesus Christ, and, if accepted, it will change a person's life.

God's proposition consists of the freedom of forgiveness and the ability to forgive others, the development of character qualities that are beyond human understanding, and the power of God to live an eternal life that begins here on earth. In addition, His proposition will give you a life of purpose beyond any other.

When God is demonstrating His life through us, it becomes obvious to others around us. As one person said to me, "You are different. What makes you different? I need to know more." Luke 17:21 says, "the Kingdom of God is within you," and His presence is in the form of the Holy Spirit, the Spirit of Christ. In Romans 12:1–2 the Apostle Paul shares the following challenge (emphasis mine):

> And so, dear brothers and sisters, I plead with you to give your bodies to God because of all he has done for you. Let them be a living and holy sacrifice—the kind he will find acceptable. This is truly the way to worship him. Don't copy the behavior and customs of this world, **but let God transform you into a new person by changing <u>the way you think</u>**. Then you will learn to know God's will for you, which is good and pleasing and perfect *(NLT)*.

This is a summary of the Spirit-filled life, and we should ask the question as to why this challenge takes courage to follow. It takes courage to be different from those around you who demand that you behave and think like them. Peer pressure can be a powerful demotivator to living the Christian life.

When I resigned from my first professional job as a high school teacher after six terrific years of teaching and coaching to engage with a Christian ministry, the principal, with whom I had a great relationship, asked the following question: "Why are you leaving? You are one of the best teachers I have. The only people I know who have gone into ministry did it because they couldn't do anything else!"

That question has caused me to reflect on what is missing in how we demonstrate what it means to be a Christian, and especially how we must communicate the greatest message ever delivered to humankind.

The passage in Romans 12:1–2 challenges us in the following ways:

- Your body and soul belong to God when you offer them in His service. God will protect His investment in you, and I believe He will give you the *courage* to be obedient.

- Always give thanks as an expression of worship for what He has done and is doing for you. It takes *courage* to be truly thankful in all circumstances, especially when things don't go as planned.

- Let God transform your thinking to think with His mind, His heart, and His values. Discipline the way you think. This will bring peace of mind, but it takes *courage* not to jump in and take over.

- Don't live and behave according to the vision and values of the world. Live according to God's purpose—love and serve one another. It takes *courage* and energy to serve others, and we tend to protect ourselves from getting hurt emotionally and physically—rejection and exhaustion.

- If you desire to know God's will, then this is the way God will reveal it to you. It takes *courage* to take the first step of faith. God will show you the rest.

The ability to influence others is based on trust. How do we build trust with the people we engage with on a regular basis? These include our family, our workmates, our church community, our neighbours, the people who serve us on a daily basis. This is not just a theory; it is about a life of action. The Apostle Paul again gives us some insights in Romans 12:6–18:

> In his grace, God has given us different gifts for doing certain things well. So, if God has given you the ability to prophesy, speak out with as much faith as God has given you. If your gift is serving others, serve them well. If you are a teacher, teach well. If your gift is to encourage others, be encouraging. If it is giving, give generously. If God has given you leadership ability, take the responsibility seriously. And if you have a gift for showing kindness to others, do it gladly.
>
> Don't just pretend to love others. Really love them. Hate what is wrong. Hold tightly to what is good. Love each other with genuine affection and take delight in honoring each other. Never be lazy but work hard and serve the Lord enthusiastically. Rejoice in our confident hope. Be patient in trouble and keep on praying. When God's people are in need, be ready to help them. Always be eager to practice hospitality.
>
> Bless those who persecute you. Don't curse them; pray that God will bless them. Be happy with those who are happy, and weep with those who weep. Live in harmony with each other. Don't be too proud to enjoy the company of ordinary people. And don't think you know it all!
>
> Never pay back evil with more evil. Do things in such a way that everyone can see you are honorable. Do all that you can to live in peace with everyone *(NLT)*.

Serving Others Through a Well-Defined Organizational Structure and the Effective Delegation of Responsibility

God did not miss anything when He instructed Moses in the basics of management. In Exodus 18:13–26, Moses was paid a visit by his father-in-law, who watched him perform his leadership duties.

Jethro, known as the Priest of Midian, was pleased to hear what the Lord had done for the Israelites and praised God for their deliverance from Egypt. Jethro even scarified a burnt offering as an act of worship to the God of the Israelites.

What happened the following day, through Jethro's observation, I like to describe as the first management seminar in biblical history, and it became the foundation for every management principle since.

There are ten principles of management and leadership development numbered in the passage (numbering and emphasis mine), which I will summarize.

> The next day Moses took his seat to serve as judge for the people, and they stood around him from morning till evening. When his father-in-law saw all that Moses was doing for the people, he said, "What is this you are doing for the people? Why do you [1] **alone** sit as judge, while all these [2] **people stand around you from morning till evening**?" Moses answered him, "Because the people come to me to seek God's will. Whenever they have a dispute, it is brought to me, and [3] **I decide between the parties and inform them of God's decrees and instructions**." Moses' father-in-law replied, "What you are doing is not good. You and these people who come to [4] **you will only wear yourselves** out. The work is too heavy for you; you cannot handle it alone. Listen now to me and I will give you some advice, and may God be with you.

You must be the people's representative before God and bring their disputes to him. [5] **Teach them his decrees and instructions, and show them the way they are to live and how they are to behave**. [6] **But select capable men from all the people—men who fear God, trustworthy men who hate dishonest gain—and appoint them as officials** [7] over thousands, hundreds, fifties and tens.

[8] Have them serve as judges for the people at all times, but have them bring every difficult case to you; the **simple cases they can decide themselves. That will make your load lighter, because they will share it with you**. If you do this and God so commands, [9] **you will be able to stand the strain, and all these people will go home satisfied**."

[10] **Moses listened to his father-in-law and did everything he said**. He chose capable men from all Israel and made them leaders of the people, officials over thousands, hundreds, fifties and tens. They served as judges for the people at all times. The difficult cases they brought to Moses, but the simple ones they decided themselves (Ex. 18:13–24*)*.

Ten Principles of Management:

1. Moses became a bottleneck because he tried to do the job by himself.

2. The people, Moses's clients, were frustrated and not well served.

3. The false premise that only the "top" of the organization can dispense God's wisdom creates a "lazy" organization waiting

for the "top" to give an answer to another person's problem. Teaching people how to mature in their levels of authority is a key principle of leadership development. The definition of authority from Dr. Adizes is *the legal right and obligation to say "yes" and "no" in the decision-making process.*

4. The stress of work can kill you if you are not delegating effectively.

5. Teach others to make decisions based on God's will. This is the same principle that Paul shared with his disciple Timothy in 2 Timothy 2:2, "And the things you have heard me say in the presence of many witnesses entrust to reliable people who will also be qualified to teach others."

6. Choose carefully to whom you will delegate. Faithful people, who fear God. People who are responsible, accountable, and know how to handle authority.

7. Delegate the size of the responsibility and authority of the role you are asking them to perform based on their maturity and the trust that you have in them.

8. Establish a rhythm with your key leadership that allows them to report the results and allows them to ask for advice from you.

9. The results will WOW the client and allow you to sleep at night!

10. Remain teachable. If you stop learning today, you will stop leading tomorrow.

We have a responsibility to help shape the future by leaving a legacy of well-trained leaders in our place. This takes a focused purpose, the energy to deal with the challenges that people bring into our lives, and the courage to serve others.

You cannot train leaders through theory alone. You must allow them the opportunity to lead. Let them build confidence in leadership through increased responsibility and authority. Create an environment around them that provides learning, coaching, and mentoring. Believe in them! Empower them to become more than you could ever be.

It will take courage, but as Jesus said to His fearful disciples during a storm on the lake, "Don't be afraid," he said. "Take courage. I am here!" (*Living Bible*, Mark 6:51).

CHAPTER 8:

Building a Foundation of Trust

I HAVE OFTEN ASKED PEOPLE, "HOW LONG DOES it take to develop trust with another person?" Most will say a long time, but if we believe that leadership is about influencing others to act, then we need to discover a way to develop trust within a shorter timeframe.

Is it possible to build trust with a person within a twenty-minute timeframe? I learned this principle when I was with the Christian Embassy in Ottawa and had the opportunity to meet with members of Parliament and ambassadors from foreign countries. For the first appointment, I was offered a brief meeting of twenty minutes due to their hectic schedule. During these meetings, my goal was to add value to the person with whom I was meeting. This had two purposes; first, it was my intention to add value from a Christian perspective, and secondly, I wanted to build trust such that I would have the opportunity for additional appointments in the future.

In order to add value to a person, it is important to listen to what they have to say. This requires you to ask effective questions, and for that you need to do some background research on the person with whom you are meeting.

I recall a first meeting with a newly elected member of Parliament, a former mayor of a small town in rural Canada. He became well-known as a result of his leadership during a serious rail accident that killed forty-seven people in his community while he was the mayor. I studied his background before I attempted to meet with him.

He welcomed me warmly into his office, as I mentioned that I was visiting him on behalf of the Christian Embassy. At this point in my career, I had become a change management associate with the Adizes organization while volunteering some time to the Christian Embassy in Ottawa. Following a brief introduction, I soon noticed his bookshelf was prominent with leadership material from John Maxwell and the Disney Corporation.

I mentioned his inspirational leadership while he was mayor, and asked if the material from Maxwell and Disney Corp. was helpful during that time. He responded with, "I love the writings of John Maxwell, and my management training with Disney was very helpful!" We found common ground in John Maxwell, as I daily enjoy his *Leadership Promises for Every Day* devotional. We were soon talking about management and leadership principles, and I found myself drawing and explaining the Lifecycle of Organizations diagram as illustrated below in Diagram 8.1.

The diagram illustrates the four roles of management at each stage by the size of the PAEI letters in the growing and ageing phases. You may note that Prime is well balanced in all four roles and ageing occurs when the organization begins to lose the entrepreneurial, E. The creative entrepreneurial role always produces more effective production, P, and when E is diminished the other three roles follow and the result is an ageing organization.

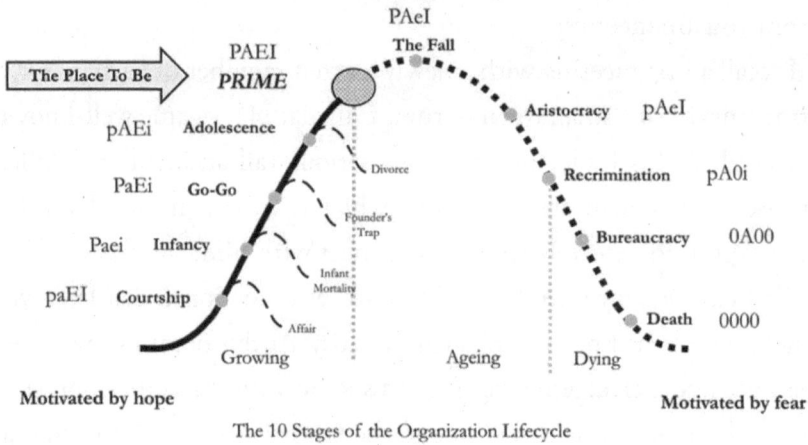

Diagram 8:1 The 10 Stages of the Organizational Lifecycle

PAeI

PAEI
PRIME

The Fall

The Place To Be

pAEi   Adolescence

PaEi   Go-Go

Paei   Infancy

paEI   Courtship

Divorce

Founder's
Trap

Infant
Mortality

Affair

Growing

Aristocracy   pAeI

Recrimination   pA0i

Bureaucracy   0A00

Death   0000

Ageing   Dying

Motivated by hope

Motivated by fear

The 10 Stages of the Organization Lifecycle

From: Managing Corporate Lifecycles by Dr. Ichak Adizes (Prentice Hall, Englewood Cliffs, NJ:)

This was a wonderful conversation until he asked me what this had to do with the Christian Embassy whom I was representing when I visited him. Now my mind was spinning with an answer to his question. I quickly shared my background with the Christian Embassy and mentioned I was now in Ottawa as a volunteer assisting them in meeting new members of Parliament. At the same time, I was asking the Lord how I should answer this question that I had never been asked before.

I told him that PRIME is the ideal place to be in your personal journey as a Christian. This is where you have a direct relationship with God, as expressed in 1 John 1:7: "But if we walk in the light, as he is in the light, we have fellowship with one another, and the blood of Jesus, his Son, purifies us from all sin."

I shared the Gospel with him briefly and spoke about the need for forgiveness from the Lord. I mentioned that when you are born again, the Holy Spirit enters your life and your journey with God takes on full meaning. I went on to share why the Holy Spirit came. Scripture mentions two things, to glorify Jesus Christ and to lead into all truth.

Having the experience of working on Parliament Hill for eleven years, two of those as chief of staff to a cabinet minister, I knew something of the pressure that a member of Parliament faces from visiting delegations whose motivation is often to convince them how to vote on one issue or another. I know that he might receive a delegation at 10:00 a.m. suggesting he vote one way on an issue and at 11:00 a.m. he may receive another with the exact opposite perspective.

I suggested that every person in a leadership position should know what truth is. The source of truth that we can trust comes from God, and it is shared in several manifestations when we have a relationship with Him. I asked him how he would know the truth and understand how to discern the motive behind what he was being told. What was his intuition telling him, and what insights did he have from previous experiences? I finished the explanation by telling him that the resources that God has for us as leaders is infinite when we are walking closely with Him, and I defined that as being in PRIME on the personal Lifecycle, to which he asked, "How can I become a Christian?"

Those resources are available to all of us as Christians, and the more we understand the practical aspects of truth, the more effective we will be in our leadership. The following is a summary of the manifestations of truth that are available to each of us who walk with the Lord.

We are promised **wisdom**:

Solomon, the wise author of the book of Proverbs in the Bible, gives us a very clear preamble as to where wisdom comes from:

> The proverbs of Solomon, son of David, king of Israel: for gaining wisdom and instruction; for understanding words of insight; for receiving instruction in prudent behavior, doing what is right and just and fair; for giving prudence to those who are simple, knowledge and discretion to the young—let the wise listen and add to their learning, and let the discerning get guidance—for understanding proverbs and parables, the sayings and riddles of the wise. The fear of the Lord is

the beginning of knowledge, but fools despise wisdom and instruction (Prov. 1:1–7).

Note in James 1:5 we are told, "If any of you lacks wisdom, you should ask God, who gives generously to all without finding fault, and it will be given to you."

With wisdom comes **discernment**:

Discernment has to do with being able to see or hear something that may or may not have been said. In terms of relationships, I like to define discernment as "listening between the lines," which can mean understanding what has not been said and being able to ask the right questions in order to clarify what you are sensing.

With discernment comes **intuition**:

Intuition is a gift from God that shows up in our lives with what we like to call "gut reaction." It is a "feeling" that can move us in making a right decision or evaluating motive.

It is a by-product of discernment and because we are made in the image of God and walking with Him in the power of the Holy Spirit, this gift can be strengthened the more we spend time with the Lord in meditation (study) and prayer.

If we are not walking with God, we need to be careful regarding our gut feelings as it says in Judges 21:25; "In those days Israel had no king; everyone did as they saw fit."

For Christian leaders, the principles of biblical truth are essential. John Maxwell makes the following comment, "Leaders must practice discernment. Relationships can get messy; people often harbor personal agendas and attempt to mask their true motives or to make them sound more noble than they really are." He goes on to say, "Leaders must read the people then lead the people. They must understand the timing, the people, the situation, and the priorities, then act accordingly."[8]

Jesus promises that we will know the **truth**:

In John 16:13–15, Jesus has this to say about the source of truth (emphasis mine):

But when He, the **Spirit of truth**, comes, **he will guide you into all the truth**. He will not speak on his own; he will speak only what he hears, and he will tell you what is yet to come. **He will glorify Me because it is from Me that he will receive what he will make known to you**. All that belongs to the Father is mine. That is why I said the Spirit will receive from me what he will make known to you.

When we become Christians, we have full-time access to the Holy Spirit if we maintain our fellowship with Jesus Christ. It is the Holy Spirit, the Spirit of Christ, who indwells each one of us who believe. This life within is the key to everything we do as Christians. In John 15:5, Jesus says, "I am the vine; you are the branches. If you remain in Me and I in you, you will bear much fruit; apart from Me you can do nothing."

If we regard all that we do that is worthwhile as "fruit," then we will quickly realize that this abiding process is the key to our success because truth is discerned by the presence of Christ in our lives in the form of His Holy Spirit. He teaches us what is worthwhile and what is not.

There is one more truth that we need to be aware of as we reflect on the relationships we have with people. The Bible has this to say:

> Those who let themselves be controlled by their lower natures live only to please themselves, but those who follow after the Holy Spirit find themselves doing those things that please God. Following after the Holy Spirit leads to life and peace, but following after the old nature leads to death because the old sinful nature within us is against God. It never did obey God's laws and it never will. That's why those who are still under the control of their old sinful selves, bent on

following their old evil desires, can never please God (*LB*, Rom. 8:5–8).

Human nature is not inherently good and getting better, as much as modern-day humanists want us to believe. Human nature is inherently sinful. If this were not the case, then there would be no reason for Christ to die on the cross for our sins. We could earn our good standing with God through whatever we consider to be worthwhile based on our humanistic beliefs. Why am I telling you this? Leaders need to be aware of the tendencies of human nature. Jesus makes the point in John 2:24–25. "But Jesus didn't trust them, for he knew mankind to the core. No one needed to tell him how changeable human nature is!" (*LB*).

We must continually ask the Lord for His truth, wisdom, and discernment when we are dealing with people.

Truth is expressed with **insight**:

One of the definitions for insight is the capacity to gain an accurate and deep intuitive understanding of a person or thing (discernment with experience). It is related to discernment, but it has the added value that comes from experience. For example, if we are to discern a behaviour that we have seen before, then the experience of seeing it previously will confirm our intuition about that person or event.

Throughout the forty-year journey to the Promised Land, Moses's leadership would be tested over and over again. In addition to understanding the truth, which came from his relationship with God as expressed in Exodus 33:11, "The Lord would speak to Moses, face to face, as one speaks to a friend," what else do we need to know that was in Moses's leadership toolbox that made him so effective?

Early on in the journey of the Exodus, and following the sin of the golden calf, Moses demonstrated his understanding as to what the real focus of his leadership was all about. Moses understood that leadership was about serving others, and when he heard God express that He would no longer accompany the Israelites on the rest of the journey, Moses moved into action. Through intercession, he again pleaded with

God on the basis of God's character in Exodus 33. When Moses heard the Lord say in Exodus 33:1–3 (emphasis mine):

> Leave this place, you and the people you brought up out of Egypt, and go up to the land I promised on oath to Abraham, Isaac and Jacob, saying, "I will give it to your descendants…" Go up to the land flowing with milk and honey. **But I will not go with you,** because you are a stiff-necked people and I might destroy you on the way.

> Moses responded, "You have been telling me, 'Lead these people,' but you have not let me know whom you will send with me. You have said, 'I know you by name and you have found favor with me.' If you are pleased with me, teach me your ways so I may know you and continue to find favor with you. Remember that this nation is your people."

> The Lord replied, "My Presence will go with you, and I will give you rest."

> Again, Moses responded, "If your Presence does not go with us, do not send us up from here. **How will anyone know that you are pleased with me and with your people unless you go with us? What else will distinguish me and your people from all the other people on the face of the earth?"**

> And the Lord said to Moses, "I will do the very thing you have asked, because I am pleased with you and I know you by name."

Putting others first is a key principle of leadership, but we must understand why this was so significant based on Moses's understanding of the purpose that he was instructed to fulfill. That purpose was to get the Israelites to the Promised Land. Why was this so important in the history of humankind?

To be an effective leader, you must always place the development of the people you are leading into the context of where you are taking them, and understand why that is so important. You must always think beyond this generation to the next, and believe that what you are doing is the fulfillment of a legacy for yourself and for the generation of people you are leading. Never stop asking yourself, "Is what I am doing worth the applied energy in the long term?" The only way you can answer that is to see the value in people development as much as what it is that you are trying to accomplish.

The Israelites were God's chosen people, but for what purpose? It was God's intention that through the Israelite people a Messiah would be born, the Son of God, to redeem humankind to Himself.

Did Moses understand all this? Do we always understand God's purpose for our lives, especially as it involves God's overall purpose for humankind? He certainly understood the unconditional promises of God when he wrote the book of Genesis. He understood the need for forgiveness when God gave him the Law and the Ten Commandments. Did he see himself as an essential part of the fulfillment of God's plan for the sacrifice of the Lamb of God for the sins of humankind that was to come through the nation of Israel? I don't believe God gave him the full picture, but his obedience to what God gave him to do was enough to allow him the endurance and perseverance regardless of the opposition that he faced from God's enemies and from the very people he was leading.

His obedience to God was based on trust. Trust was the foundation of his relationship with God, just as it is with you and me. Faith in God is the foundation of our Christian life, but before we understand the power of faith in God and all that is available to us, we must first experience the delight of despair.

CHAPTER 9:

The Delight of Despair

MY ZOOM CALL THIS MORNING WITH BIBLES and Bros. at 6:00 a.m. was a heavy one. The focus of the conversation was despair and what the Lord is doing in our lives when we encounter it.

This is a one-hour video call every Tuesday and Thursday morning for a group of men from all walks of life and experience to tell what God is doing in their lives. It is a thoughtful, refreshing time as a group of brothers share, with great freedom, their lives of faith and how it applies to the challenges of being a Christian in today's world.

Following the call, I read Oswald Chambers' daily devotional, *My Utmost for His Highest* from May 24. I read this and other devotionals every morning as well as a chapter of Scripture, taking notes in a journal based on what I believe the Lord is saying to me. The title of Chambers' devotional was "The Delight of Despair," and it gave me pause to reflect on how I have dealt with discouragement, disappointment, and rejection at different times in my life, just as Moses faced in the forty-year journey leading the Israelites in the wilderness.

When I agreed to take on the role of chief of staff to a cabinet minister in the Canadian federal government in early 1991, I knew there would be challenges in fitting in with others who performed the same role with other ministers. Many of them came through the political system defined by loyalty to the minister, the grunt work involved in winning elections, and the ability to build a network of trusted, like-minded support. This was not true for me, as my main qualification was being a friend of the minister who had known my work directing the Christian Embassy for seven years, and together we supported a value system based on Christian principles.

Democracies are built on the principle of the right of descension, which stimulates the debate required to respect the input of dissenting views. It is an adversarial system that is intended to stimulate discussion from differing viewpoints to create the best decision possible for the people that the political institutions represent.

However, it seldom works out that way. The more fixed a political party is in their position, based on their perspective or worldview, the more they are resistant to input from others. Political adversarial systems are not always open to dialogue or input. When this happens, the required culture of mutual trust and respect disintegrates. Personal agendas and pride rule the day, resulting in a culture of conflict. In many ways, it is the anthesis of the Christian values of peacemaking and being of service to others. This was the environment that I entered when I became the chief of staff for the minister.

I would meet with all the chiefs of staff every Wednesday morning to discuss the priority issues for each of our departments as they impacted the overall government agenda. The consistent viewpoint focused on the government always being right and the opposition was always unrealistic and naïve. In some ways, I felt like an outsider, and I had much to learn in developing a sense of credibility within the system.

After being in the position for several months, I was delighted to read an article that defined my minister's team as being one of the best run offices on Parliament Hill. Much of the credit belonged to the minister, the previous chiefs of staff, and the team themselves based on their loyalty to the minister and their outstanding efforts to fulfill their responsibilities. I was blessed to lead a group of people who had each other's backs, and it was my job to keep it running smoothly with the best interests of the minister and the government in mind.

Later in my tenure, I was to read a newspaper article that assumed to rate the performance of the chiefs of staff on the hill, and it was not very kind to me, based on the reporter's evaluation. As much as I felt fulfilled in the job I was doing and was especially pleased with the performance of the staff, I immediately felt discouragement and rejection.

Looking back, I am surprised by how short a time it took from feelings of satisfaction based on believing I was doing a good job to thinking that somehow, I was a failure. I internalized the whole thing, which resulted in being irrational in how I viewed myself. I wanted to defend myself. I was even thinking about calling the reporter who wrote the article based on the input of other chiefs of staff and who never once talked to me or my team to gain a different perspective. My other surprise was how long it took for me to share my feelings with the Lord, even though I was walking with Him daily.

Self-esteem is a powerful motivator or demotivator, and I will always appreciate the words of encouragement from my minister and two others ministers who offered words of support.

I learned a lot from this episode in my career as a leader. Not the least of which is the understanding of how well the Lord is acquainted with my comings and goings as it says in Psalm 139:3, "You scrutinize my path and my lying down, And You are intimately acquainted with all my ways" (*Amplified Bible*). The Lord knows what is going on in my life and what I am dealing with at any point in time. How do I remain content during the times that I am troubled by those who devalue the role of God in our lives?

1 Timothy 6:6–7 is an encouragement meant for such times as these:

Perpetual friction between men who are corrupted in mind and deprived of the truth, who think that godliness is a source of profit [a lucrative, money-making business—withdraw from them]. But godliness actually is a source of great gain when accompanied by contentment [that contentment which comes from a sense of inner confidence based on the sufficiency of God] (*AB*).

God is our source for contentment and truth, and He is always open to a discussion with us at any time during our days to offer wisdom and a sense of peace, His peace (Matt. 11:28).

My personality has a strong presence of the I, Integrator management style (which I described in Chapter Two). I have a strong people focus, which works very well for me when I am involved in team building, but the downside is a tendency to be overly introspective. When criticized, I find it difficult to learn from it, forget it, and move on.

Once I sought the Lord, He reminded me of 2 Corinthians 7:6, that He is in the business of comforting the downcast, and often through others who know me well. I was especially filled with joy when I read Psalm 94:19, "When anxiety was great within me, your consolation brought me joy."

What I have learned through my experiences and through the study of Moses's leadership is that we must operate in a world of unbelief where ego is manifest, and people enjoy bringing others down to their carnal level. It took Moses some time to learn how to manage the opposition he faced that came from people who preferred the status quo and the comforts of the past rather than making the commitments necessary to follow God and appreciate what He was doing in rescuing them from slavery. Not everyone wanted Moses to succeed, and there are those out there who don't want you to succeed either, which is often a measure of their own insecurities.

There was a point in the life of Moses when he shared his frustration with God. Exodus 5:22–23 describes the despair that Moses was feeling when he and his brother confronted Pharaoh with no more result than an increased workload on the Hebrew slaves.

> Moses returned to the Lord and said, "Why, Lord, why have you brought trouble on this people? Is this why you sent me? Ever since I went to Pharaoh to speak in your name, he has brought trouble on this people, and you have not rescued your people at all."

From a human perspective, we can understand how he felt. He grew up believing he was to lead the Israelites to the Promised Land; he acted on his own strength at age forty and was forced to flee into the desert. He looked after sheep for his father-in-law for forty years, and then he was asked by God to fulfill a calling which he—reluctantly and full of doubt—accepted. He then travelled to Egypt to confront Pharaoh, who immediately rejected the proposal to free the people and increased the Hebrew workload based on his unbelief and pride. This again resulted in Moses's own people rejecting his leadership, which brought back memories of despair that he had felt forty years earlier. Moses's worst fears were being realized!

I believe that at some point in our lives we all feel despair in varying degrees, especially when our hopes are dashed and we are filled with disappointment. Faith in God is not always our default decision-making position in life because our human nature channels us into thinking we can solve most things that come our way, and our default becomes self-effort. The failure of our self-effort can, and often does, lead to despair. Our response does not lead us to take responsibility for failure; rather, we somehow want to blame someone or something else. As Christians, we often end up blaming God, just like Moses did.

In Matthew 11:28–30, we are made aware of God's response to our dilemma:

Come to me, all you who are weary and burdened, and I will give you rest. Take my yoke upon you and learn from me, for I am gentle and humble in heart, and you will find rest for your souls. For my yoke is easy and my burden is light.

God answers our desire for retribution and vengeance with His love. As the Son of Man, Jesus understood every emotion that we face, especially rejection. He is fully aware of how to deal with our despair and provides the renewal of hope that we are desperately looking for.

How did God answer Moses when he had come to the end of himself? Exodus 6:1 says, "Then the Lord said to Moses, 'Now you will see what I will do to Pharaoh: Because of my mighty hand he will let them go; because of my mighty hand he will drive them out of his country.'"

God is the One who will bring the results. He wants to use us, but only when we realize He is the One who will provide the power and the resources to make it happen. Only when we humble ourselves before the Lord will we understand how awesome our relationship is with Jesus Christ. We can accomplish the things that He calls us to do as long as we maintain our role in a proper perspective with His.

Throughout the remainder of the forty years that it took to reach the Promised Land, Moses would face the challenge of rebellion and disappointment many times over. Only once, toward the end of the journey, did he allow his frustrations to get the better of him. In the next chapter, I will summarize how Moses dealt with his emotions based on the dynamic relationship that he had with a Living God, the same God we are able to walk with daily.

CHAPTER 10:

We Will Never Walk Alone

T HE EVENTS DESCRIBED IN THE LAST VERSES of Exodus 5 and God's response to Moses in Exodus 6 were a turning point for Moses in his relationship with God and his leadership of the Israelites. The realization that the Christian life cannot be fulfilled according to God's purposes without a total commitment to God Himself and a dependence on His resources may not come as a surprise to you, but I hope it will be a turning point for you.

Being born again was the beginning of our journey with God. For Wendy and me, this was a whole new experience when God sought us out and convinced us that we needed to have a relationship with Him. As we matured in our faith journey, we developed an increase of trust on our walk with God, and we appreciated the adventures that He had in mind for us. Our initial decisions were genuine, but we really didn't know much about where we were going in life either from a career or spiritual perspective.

Quite often, the career path takes over our sense of responsibilities and our spiritual development gets left behind.

On the next page, Diagram 10.1 illustrates the various phases of the personal Lifecycle that, I believe, we will all experience in one way or another as we journey through life. The solid black line represents the growing phases and the dashed line, the Ageing phases.

The descriptions of the ten phases of the personal Lifecycle reflect our life journey beginning with Dreaming and moving toward Significance as the ideal goal of what we are trying to achieve in our walk with the Lord. Each phase focuses on questions that we asked ourselves during this timeframe.

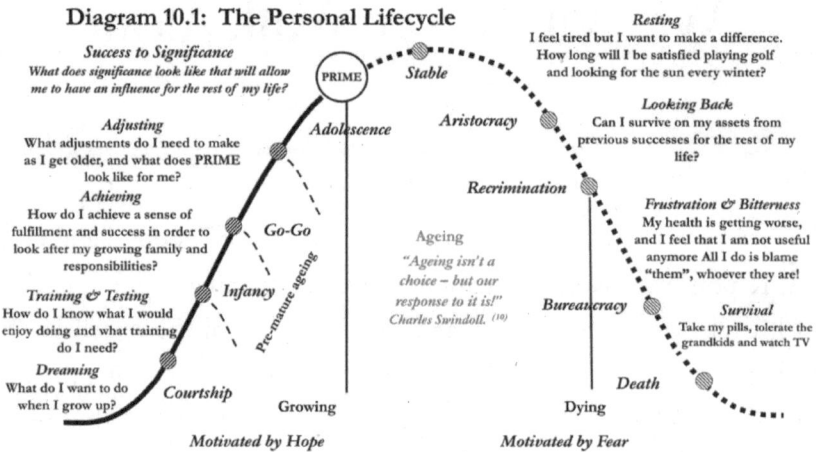

Diagram 10.1: The Personal Lifecycle

Success to Significance
What does significance look like that will allow me to have an influence for the rest of my life?

Adjusting
What adjustments do I need to make as I get older, and what does PRIME look like for me?

Achieving
How do I achieve a sense of fulfillment and success in order to look after my growing family and responsibilities?

Training & Testing
How do I know what I would enjoy doing and what training do I need?

Dreaming
What do I want to do when I grow up?

PRIME
Adolescence
Go-Go
Infancy
Courtship

Pre-mature ageing

Growing

Motivated by Hope

Stable
Aristocracy
Recrimination

Ageing
"Ageing isn't a choice – but our response to it is!"
Charles Swindoll. [10]

Bureaucracy

Dying

Motivated by Fear

Resting
I feel tired but I want to make a difference. How long will I be satisfied playing golf and looking for the sun every winter?

Looking Back
Can I survive on my assets from previous successes for the rest of my life?

Frustration & Bitterness
My health is getting worse, and I feel that I am not useful anymore All I do is blame "them", whoever they are!

Survival
Take my pills, tolerate the grandkids and watch TV

Death

The dashed line represents the Ageing phases of life, which I do not believe we have to experience. I am well aware that as our bodies get older, they begin to disintegrate at various rates to the point that they cannot sustain life. However, I don't believe it is necessary to move beyond PRIME as long as we are able to maintain a positive attitude and a positive relationship with God.

The comments offered in the Ageing phases come from my interaction with people who are experiencing the frustrations of getting old, with some feeling that they have nothing more to contribute.

The Growing phases are motivated by "hope" and the Ageing phases are motivated by "fear." *The Lifecycle journey does not depend on your age.* Some people tend to display the characteristics of ageing at a much younger age than others because their lives are filled with stress brought on by the challenges of life. Still others are motivated to continue to make a difference well beyond what is considered to be retirement age. The questions I would like to ask you are: "What difference does a relationship with God have on your outlook on life, and what difference does having a purpose make on maintaining a positive attitude?"

Diagram 10.2 defines our spiritual journey on the Lifecycle and its inconsistencies between growing and searching.

The wavy line, often referred to as a roller coaster, describes the stages that we have gone through in our spiritual lives. When that line moves to the inside of the bell curve, these represent times of searching for spiritual truth, or times where our spiritual lives have lost their focus.

10.2 i: As soon as we became spiritually conscious of the existence of God, we became curious as to what that meant for us.

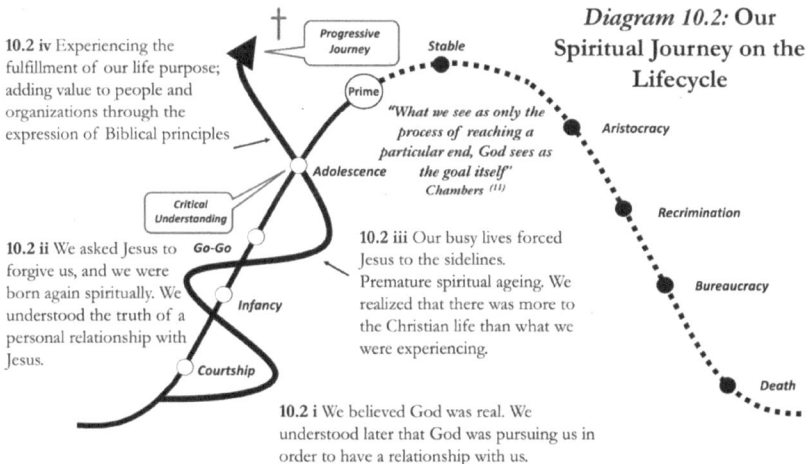

10.2 iv Experiencing the fulfillment of our life purpose; adding value to people and organizations through the expression of Biblical principles

Progressive Journey

Stable

Prime

Diagram 10.2: **Our Spiritual Journey on the Lifecycle**

"What we see as only the process of reaching a particular end, God sees as the goal itself" Chambers [11]

Aristocracy

Adolescence

Critical Understanding

Recrimination

10.2 ii We asked Jesus to forgive us, and we were born again spiritually. We understood the truth of a personal relationship with Jesus.

Go-Go

Infancy

10.2 iii Our busy lives forced Jesus to the sidelines. Premature spiritual ageing. We realized that there was more to the Christian life than what we were experiencing.

Bureaucracy

Courtship

Death

10.2 i We believed God was real. We understood later that God was pursuing us in order to have a relationship with us.

That started for me when I was part of the Sunday School program at my local church (1953–59), and for Wendy it began when she was very young and wanted to be assured of the Lord's presence in her life. Being curious about God and knowing Him personally are two different things.

We became aware of this when we visited my sister in California in August 1968, which resulted in our asking Jesus Christ for forgiveness and inviting Him into our hearts to become born again (John 3).

10.2 ii: Being convinced that we were separated from a relationship with God, we asked Him for forgiveness. Our initial commitment to Him allowed us to be born again and to begin our journey with the Lord.

10.2 iii: This describes our spiritual condition once we entered the hectic Go-Go stage of our lives where personal interests became a priority such that we pushed aside a growth plan that would allow us to mature as Christians. This was not intentional, but daily routine, personal objectives, and a growing family took over our priorities. We were not even aware that we needed a spiritual wake-up call!

In the New Testament, the Apostle Paul writes the following:

> Dear friends, you always followed my instructions when I was with you. And now that I am away, it is even more important. Work hard to show the results of your salvation, obeying God with deep reverence and fear. For God is working in you, giving you the desire and the power to do what pleases him (*NLT*, Phil. 2:12–13).

This passage refers to the fact that we need to work out what God has placed in us. I can never get over the fact that Jesus comes to dwell within us through the presence of the Holy Spirit. We become the temple of God! This is a relational experience, one where the nature and character of Jesus shapes our character to become like His. The verses also say we are to work out in our lives His character in all that we do as a life of reverence, *based on our trust* in Him. Jesus wants to live His life through us. WOW!

10.2 iv: This describes that awakening. It defines the life of a disciple, committed and sold out to the Lord in order to do His will.

In this phase, there were two things that came together for Wendy and me, and they were a practical understanding of the role of the Holy Spirit in our lives and a commitment to a purpose worth living for. It was in this phase that we made some life decisions that took us on a new career path that required total trust in the Lord for every aspect of our lives, including financial security and the well-being of our family. God never let us down!

Our maturing process was provided through good churches and practical teaching that allowed us to maintain our relationship with the Lord on an ongoing basis.

We were taught something called "spiritual breathing." Allow me to explain why this is so significant in maintaining our relationship with God.

There is a difference between having a relationship with someone, such as father and son, and experiencing the joy of fellowship with that same person.

When God's Holy Spirit enters our life and we are walking with the Lord, we are constantly faced with temptation, which only becomes a real problem if we yield to that temptation. A promise of God found in 1 Corinthians 10:13 tells us that it is not necessary to sin when you are walking with the Lord and listening for His voice within you, which has a direct impact on your conscience:

> No temptation has overtaken you except what is common to mankind. And God is faithful; he will not let you be tempted beyond what you can bear. But when you are tempted, he will also provide a way out so that you can endure it.

However, if you do fall short, it is necessary to ask for forgiveness and once again re-establish your fellowship with God. Herein lies the principle of spiritual breathing. Exhaling is asking for forgiveness for disappointing our Lord, or offending others, and inhaling is asking Him to re-establish His fellowship with us. Often, the Lord will direct us to attempt to regain trust with the people that we have offended.

Jesus promises that He will never leave us or forsake us. He did not depart from His relationship with us when we demonstrated poor behaviour; we just chose not to listen to Him or take His advice when we faced temptation. The more we continue to go our own way and don't admit that we are wrong, when we know we are, the more difficult it is to overcome our own pride, or even consider that God has our best interests at the centre of His heart.

As a result, our fellowship with God is broken.

The command of God is that we be filled with the Holy Spirit as given to us in Scripture in Ephesians 5:18. "Be filled with the Spirit. And do not get drunk with wine, for that is dissipation (self-indulgence), but be filled with the Spirit."

The Lord also gives us the promise that He will always answer when we pray according to His will.

> And this is the confidence which we have before Him, that, if we ask anything according to His will, He hears us. And if we know that He hears us in whatever we ask, we know that we have the requests which we have asked of Him (1 John 5:14–15).

The big eye opener for us was an understanding of the role that the Holy Spirit plays in the life of a believer. He loves us. He pursues us. He invites us into a son and daughter relationship with Him. He empowers us. He expects us to walk through life with Him to be co-labourers in His plans for humankind. In the Bible, God calls us His children and His desire for us is to call Him Abba, Father.

Galatians 4:6 says, "Because you are his sons, God sent the Spirit of his Son into our hearts, the Spirit who calls out, 'Abba, Father.'"

The concept of "spiritual breathing" and its application to our lives is based on the knowledge of three specific passages found in the New Testament. Ephesians 5:18 and 1 John 5:14–15 are explained above.

The third verse, found in 1 John 1:9, is especially significant if our fellowship with God is broken: "If we confess our sins, He is faithful and just and will forgive us our sins and purify us from all unrighteousness."

Why is spiritual breathing so significant in maintaining our fellowship with God? Human nature is easily tempted and it doesn't take much for us to make poor decisions, offend someone else, or demonstrate too much ego.

When the Holy Spirit speaks to our conscience, telling us that we have done something wrong, contrary to God's values, verbally abusing someone, demonstrating impatience or anger with our spouse or kids, cheating on an exam, filling out income tax forms in a questionable way, extrapolating results to make ourselves look good, or just having a bad attitude, to name a few, then we have a choice. We can either admit that what we have done is wrong and ask for forgiveness from God and those affected, or we can try to ignore what we have done by believing that it really wasn't all that serious.

Ignoring our indiscretions creates two problems: it destroys our fellowship with God because of our disobedience, and it adds to the "guilt vault" in our lives where we store the things we should or should not have done. It is easy to make a deposit in the vault, but only God can withdraw them through His forgiveness.

These inactions have consequences because the guilt doesn't easily go away, driven by the memories of not living as we want, but knowing that we should. We are not being honest with ourselves or with God, and the result is that we begin to live a deceptive life, trying to show others something that we are not.

Many people don't see this in their lives, but God does, and the result is that we begin to lose our freedom to be the person God created us to be. Living with guilt always takes internal energy to deal with, and this energy takes away the energy required to have a positive influence on the world around us.

There is great freedom in forgiveness. I especially enjoy explaining this principle to people in leadership positions, those who have considerable responsibilities with the people that report to them.

Every person needs to have the freedom to make decisions that are going to affect the lives of the people that are part of your life, and, to do that, they must be unencumbered by anything that keeps them from drawing on the power of God to assist.

Carrying a load of guilt is a major restraint to real freedom.

Not only do we need to admit our guilt, but we need to ask for forgiveness for the things that caused it in the first place, and, often, we need to make it right with the people who have been hurt.

Here is a suggested prayer that God will hear if it comes from your heart:

> *God, I have messed up. I thank you that you are willing to forgive me because of your love for me. I know that I have broken your trust, and I am asking to be forgiven. I can't live the Christian life without You, and I want to be fully committed to You with every aspect of my life. Thank you for forgiving me and for re-energizing me through the power of Your Spirit. Amen.*

Our ability to talk to God like this, shared from your heart, is the key to our Christian walk. We will face temptation. The first prayer we call on God to answer is the one that asks Him to help us through that temptation. Why would we not be in constant prayer—constant communication with God regarding everything that we face, whether problems or opportunities? He does hear, and He does answer! Our life journey is a proof of that.

What I am sharing with you is foundational for effective leadership. Our ability to lead others, whether that is through your employment or giving leadership to your family, especially the challenges that teenagers get themselves into, or a volunteer ministry that you are engaged in, all have a common focus, and that is our ability to influence others through service. This is the principle that the Apostle shared with the Philippian church in Philippians 2:3–5:

> Do nothing out of selfish ambition or vain conceit. Rather, in humility value others above yourselves, not looking to your own interests but each of you to the interests of the others. In your relationships with one another, have the same mindset as Christ Jesus *(NLT)*.

This was the focal point of Moses's success as a leader, as demonstrated in the passages that I shared with you in Chapter Eight, when he faced the rebellion that ended up with the Israelites worshipping a golden calf. Moses pleaded for the people he was leading because God was about to destroy them because of their sin and rebellion. Moses's prayer of intercession for the Israelites would not have been possible if Moses did not have a genuine heart of service for these people. He was even willing to give his own life in exchange for God forgiving the Israelites.

> So, Moses went back to the Lord and said, "Oh, what a great sin these people have committed! They have made themselves gods of gold. But now, please forgive their sin—**but if not, then blot me out of the book you have written** (Ex. 32:31–32, emphasis mine)).

In this passage, Moses is foretelling the ministry of Jesus and His willingness to forgive us based on the love that He has for humanity.

This same Spirit indwells us as believers, and it is the Spirit of a servant leader. The only way you can lead this way is if you are willing to totally depend on Christ for His wisdom and His character as demonstrated through the fruit of the Holy Spirit.

The most important decision that you will make in your leadership journey is to understand what it means to lead with the resources of the Holy Spirit. When that happens, you will be amazed with what the Lord has in store for you to accomplish and the influence you will have on the people you lead.

CHAPTER 11:

Leadership Is Complicated

JOHN MAXWELL IS AN AUTHOR AND VALUED speaker and resource to many who have studied the subject of leadership, especially from a Christian perspective. He shares the following description of leadership, which really expresses why it is so difficult to be definitive about the subject.

> The ability to lead is really a collection of skills, nearly all of which can be learned and improved. Leadership is complicated. It has many facets: respect, experience, emotional strength, people skills, discipline, vision, momentum, timing—the list goes on. Many of the factors in leadership are intangible. The learning process is ongoing, the result of self-discipline and perseverance.[9]

For these reasons, the stories of great leaders are best expressed by sharing examples from their leadership story. There is no better example than the life of Moses and in this chapter, I will try to illustrate how he persevered in the midst of the challenges he faced, most of which are described in Maxwell's definition above.

The Exodus is so much more than getting the Israelites from one geographical place to another. Within the first five books of the Bible, called the Pentateuch, are the writings of Moses as dictated to him by God.

- **Genesis:** "Genesis provides us with God's perspective on the beginnings of several key Bible issues, such as creation, marriage, sin, sacrifice and Hebrew history."[10]

- **Exodus:** "This book vividly recounts God's dramatic plan to redeem His people by raising up a deliverer, Moses, protecting the Israelites from the ten plagues, bringing them safely through the sea and providing for their needs in the wilderness."[11]

- **Leviticus:** "Leviticus teaches us that God expects more than mere lip service from those who follow Him—our lives in Christ should reflect a new quality of living. It also provides us with a mirror image of our own depravity and need for cleansing in Christ's blood."[12]

- **Numbers:** "Numbers reminds us of God's holiness and outlines the dangers of dishonoring Him by the sin of unbelief. It teaches us that, without an eternal perspective, we will live by sight rather than faith and will be unwilling to take the risks of obedience."[13]

- **Deuteronomy:** "Deuteronomy summarizes the lessons learned during Israel's Exodus and wilderness experiences. It also encourages believers today to pursue the wise course of holiness—reinforcing the truth that, in the long run, disobedience to God's Word is always more painful than obedience."[14]

Moses was a type of prophet, priest, and king in that he was a representation of the coming Christ. He was not perfect and was therefore unable to substitute himself for the sins of the people he was leading, as illustrated in Exodus 32:32, but in many other ways he was a predictor of the coming Christ.

As a prophet, he both taught and applied the Word of God as well as predicted future events concerning God's chosen people. As a priest, he communicated God's salvation and forgiveness to the Israelites as outlined in the Law of God. In his priestly function, he also demonstrated God's love, care, and provision for His people. As a king, he offered Israel an eternal perspective, not only through his leadership, but also by sharing the purpose of why this journey was necessary in the first place. As believers, we are the fulfillment of that purpose, and our responsibility is to pass it on to others.

One of the greatest attributes that we receive from the Spirit of Christ when we become Christians is self-control (Galatians 5:22–23). In positions of leadership, more is caught than taught, and believe me, people will be watching you all the time. Not everyone wants to see you succeed. If you are privileged to have children, you are likely amused when you see your children copy your behaviour and even the way you speak, at an early age. As we get older, we begin to see that modelling is a significant way of expressing who we are, and followers are evaluating you, asking, does your walk match your talk?

Self-control is the ability to control your emotional reactions during times of stress. Our temptation is to react according to our personality. For a high P, Producer style, you might respond by saying, "Why aren't you doing it the way I asked you to do it?" For a high A, Administration style, you might wonder why things are not being done according to the rules or established principles. For a high E, Entrepreneurial style, you might be frustrated by how long it is taking to implement the idea that was discussed last week. The high I, Integrator style, will be frustrated with the lack of unity in the team assigned to get the project done.

Self-control allows you to slow down and ask yourself questions based on the nine attributes of the fruits of Christ's Spirit as illustrated in Diagram 11.1.

This is a simple self-evaluation, but it will require you to think about your leadership attributes more from a values perspective than from a personality perspective. If your behaviour changes as a result of your evaluation, then this is evidence that you are filled with the Holy Spirit and working out your obedience to Him.

Diagram 11:1: Self-analysis - The Fruit of the Spirit

DISCIPLINE	SPONTANEOUS IMPACT
Am I displaying **"self control"** – in my work and with my family? *"Do I trust You Jesus, to help me to discipline myself, to share Your Spirit rather than my nature?"*	Am I displaying **"love & appreciation"** for those around me? Am I demonstrating a servant heart, willing to empower others?
	Am I receiving and experiencing a portion of Your **"joy"** Lord, YOU having been anointing with the oil of joy? (Heb. 1:9)
	Do people see me as **"peaceful"** or up-tight? Help me to be a peacemaker?
	Am I **"patient"** in my teaching and in my ability to listen before I speak? Is my patience seen as Your love flowing through me?
	Do I demonstrate **"kindness"** when people don't understand?
	Do I express Your **"goodness"** in helping them to deal with the challenges of life?
	"Am I **"faithful"** to represent You, Jesus in all my actions?"
	Do I approach people with a **"gentle"** spirit even when their performance doesn't measure up to my expectations ?

There are two incidents in Moses's leadership that look very much the same, but one is at the beginning of the Exodus journey, described in Exodus 17:1–7 and the other is toward the end of the journey, described in Numbers 20:4–12.

> The whole Israelite community set out from the Desert of Sin, traveling from place to place as the Lord commanded. They camped at Rephidim, but there was no water for the people to drink. So, they quarreled with Moses and said, "Give us water to drink." Moses

replied, "Why do you quarrel with me? Why do you put the Lord to the test?"

But the people were thirsty for water there, and they grumbled against Moses. They said, "Why did you bring us up out of Egypt to make us and our children and livestock die of thirst?" Then Moses cried out to the Lord, "What am I to do with these people? They are almost ready to stone me." The Lord answered Moses, "Go out in front of the people. Take with you some of the elders of Israel and take in your hand the staff with which you struck the Nile, and go. I will stand there before you by the rock at Horeb. Strike the rock, and water will come out of it for the people to drink." So, Moses did this in the sight of the elders of Israel. And he called the place Massah and Meribah because the Israelites quarreled and because they tested the Lord saying, "Is the Lord among us or not?" (Ex. 17:1–7).

Here we see an example of the disciplined, self-controlled action of Moses under stress, the stress of the constant complaint from the people whom he was leading. In verse 2, the people complained due to lack of water at Rephidim. Moses did not try to defend himself, but rather turned the complaint over to the Lord to remind the people that their complaint was not against him, but the Lord.

His disciplined action allowed him to see that every problem was an opportunity to trust God. Moses did not try to take his frustration out on the people, but expressed his frustration to the Lord (Exodus 17:4). As a result of this process, the Lord was able to take the request and deal with it as only the Lord could—and God was glorified.

Numbers 20 takes place toward the end of the Exodus journey. Moses's sister Miriam had died and Aaron was to die soon as well. The example illustrated in verses 1 to 13 is the result of forty years of complaints from the people Moses was leading and finally his frustration got the better of him. He lost his sense of self-discipline (emphasis mine):

> In the first month the whole Israelite community arrived at the Desert of Zin, and they stayed at Kadesh. There Miriam died and was buried
>
> Now there was no water for the community, and the people gathered in opposition to Moses and Aaron. They quarreled with Moses and said, "If only we had died when our brothers fell dead before the Lord! Why did you bring the Lord's community into this wilderness, that we and our livestock should die here? Why did you bring us up out of Egypt to this terrible place? It has no grain or figs, grapevines or pomegranates. And there is no water to drink!"
>
> Moses and Aaron went from the assembly to the entrance to the tent of meeting and fell facedown, and the glory of the Lord appeared to them. The Lord said to Moses, "Take the staff, and you and your brother Aaron gather the assembly together. **Speak to that rock** before their eyes and it will pour out its water. You will bring water out of the rock for the community so they and their livestock can drink."
>
> **So, Moses took the staff from the Lord's presence**, just as he commanded him. He and Aaron gathered the assembly together in front of the rock and Moses said to them, "Listen, you rebels, **must we bring you water out of this rock?**" Then Moses raised his arm and **struck the rock twice** with his staff. Water gushed out, and the community and their livestock drank.

But the Lord said to Moses and Aaron, "Because you did not trust in me enough to honor me as holy in the sight of the Israelites, you will not bring this community into the land I give them." These were the waters of Meribah, where the Israelites quarreled with the Lord and where he was proved holy among them (Num. 20:1–13).

The Word of God is a living document, and it is practical in the understanding of our relationship with the Lord. In addition, the Old Testament is a historical document that allows us to see God's plan for eternity and our role in it. There is much symbolism in the verses I have just illustrated, not just about our need for self-discipline. The two passages are a description of the significance of Christ as symbolized by the rock and the water flowing freely from it, which is a symbol of the Holy Spirit. In order to understand the sin that Moses and Aaron performed in Numbers 20 that did not allow them to enter the Promised Land, we must understand a previous passage in Numbers 17.

The Lord said to Moses, "Speak to the Israelites and get twelve staffs from them, one from the leader of each of their ancestral tribes. Write the name of each man on his staff. On the staff of Levi write Aaron's name, for there must be one staff for the head of each ancestral tribe. Place them in the tent of meeting in front of the ark of the covenant law, where I meet with you. The staff belonging to the man I choose will sprout, and I will rid myself of this constant grumbling against you by the Israelites."

So, Moses spoke to the Israelites, and their leaders gave him twelve staffs, one for the leader of each of their ancestral tribes, and Aaron's staff was among them.

Moses placed the staffs before the Lord in the tent of the covenant law.

The next day Moses entered the tent and saw that Aaron's staff, which represented the tribe of Levi, had not only sprouted but had budded, blossomed and produced almonds. Then Moses brought out all the staffs from the Lord's presence to all the Israelites. They looked at them, and each of the leaders took his own staff.

The Lord said to Moses, "Put back Aaron's staff in front of the ark of the covenant law, to be kept as a sign to the rebellious. This will put an end to their grumbling against me, so that they will not die." Moses did just as the Lord commanded him (Num. 17:1–11).

Aaron was a Levite of God's ordained priesthood. The Levites were responsible for offering the sacrifices, as outlined in the Law, for the sins of the people. The animal sacrifices offered to God were all about the need for forgiveness. When Christ came, He was known as the Lamb of God, the unblemished sacrifice, who alone would satisfy God's dilemma of loving humankind while requiring the redemption of sins (forgiveness) as the foundation of His relationship. This is the basis of our forgiveness today as Christians, and forgiveness is the only real path to freedom.

The twelve staffs were placed before the Lord as instructed. The next day, Aaron's staff had not only sprouted, but had budded, blossomed, and produced almonds. A dead staff comes to life and blossoms. This is a symbol of the resurrection of Christ who died on a cross, was placed in a tomb, and after three days appeared to His disciples and many others. We too will be resurrected after we die, and spend eternity with Christ Jesus in heaven.

Moses let his emotions get the better of him in carrying out God's instructions as defined in Numbers 20.

Maybe he was thinking back to the similar situation that he experienced nearly forty years earlier when he was asked to strike the rock, a symbol of Christ's death from which came "rivers of living water." God always has something to teach us and even when our situations may look the same, they do not always require the same strategy in dealing with them.

Moses and Aaron presented themselves before the Lord in order to seek His advice, which was the right thing to do, but they did not carry out God's instructions with the intention of honouring Him in the presence of the people. In a sense, they grieved the Holy Spirit.

Moses took from the tabernacle the rod of Aaron, which had budded and bloomed—the representation of the Living Christ—and used it to strike the rock, the symbol of Christ, not once, but twice! In the similar incident forty years earlier, God told Moses to strike the rock with his rod—the one he used to part the waters. This was a symbol of Christ's death on the cross.

During Christ's time on earth, the religious leaders of the day, motivated by human nature and influenced by Satan, found it more acceptable to kill Christ than believe what was revealed in the Old Testament Scriptures.

Moses was instructed to "speak to that rock before their eyes and it will pour out its water." As Christians, we have direct access to Christ, who is seated at the right hand of the Father in heaven (Ephesians 3:12) as a result of our relationship with Him and the sacrifice He made for us. There is no need for any additional substitutional offering, whether it is through the blood of bulls and goats or the work we do in order to get the Lord's attention. We have direct access now, and He intercedes for us when we don't know how we should pray. This was what was being symbolized in Numbers 20.

Moses was distracted by the rebels who did nothing complain for forty years, like we do if we lose our self-control. God disciplined him as a result of his disobedience as He will with us if we choose to ignore the lessons that He is trying to teach us.

The late Howie Hendricks, professor at Dallas Theological Seminary, said, "If you stop learning today, you will stop leading tomorrow!"[15]

CHAPTER 12:

Being Lost Can Become a Way of Life

THE STORY OF THE EXODUS IS ALSO the story of a lost generation. Over the four hundred years that the Hebrew people were in the land of Egypt as aliens, and in the later period as slaves, it is believed that they began to follow the customs and beliefs of the Egyptian culture. Many of them would have heard the story of how they got to Egypt during a time of famine, but there is a big difference between having an appreciation for the culture and having the personal faith that was demonstrated through the life of Abraham. The spiritual maturity of many who participated in the Exodus was limited.

During the first two years of their journey, the fundamentals of management were established, as explained in Chapter Seven. Management and leadership infrastructures were established that allowed the basic needs of the people to be met. In addition, rules, policies, and laws were taught that established how to live and relate to one another. They established a system of governance that would allow them to follow God's principles of leadership, management, and spiritual well-being in preparation to succeed as a society in the Promised Land given to them by God.

At the end of the two years in the wilderness, they arrived at Kadesh-Barnea, the entrance to the Promised Land. It was here that they were given the first opportunity to enter the land that was to become their heritage through whom the promised Messiah, the Son of God, was to enter the world.

The following account is given in Deuteronomy 1:19–25, (emphasis mine)

> Then, as the Lord our God commanded us, we set out from Horeb and went toward the hill country of the Amorites through all that vast and dreadful wilderness that you have seen, and so we reached Kadesh Barnea. Then I said to you, "You have reached the hill country of the Amorites, which the Lord our God is giving us. See, the Lord your God has given you the land. Go up and take possession of it as the Lord, the God of your ancestors, told you. Do not be afraid; do not be discouraged."
>
> **Then all of you came to me and said, "Let us send men ahead to spy out the land for us and bring back a report about the route we are to take and the towns we will come to."**
>
> The idea seemed good to me; so, I selected twelve of you, one man from each tribe. They left and went up into the hill country, and came to the Valley of Eshkol and explored it. Taking with them some of the fruit of the land, they brought it down to us and reported, "It is a good land that the Lord our God is giving us."

The suggestion to send spies into the land was made by the leaders from the twelve tribes. They wanted to do, what we call today, due diligence. As Numbers 13:1 says, "The Lord said to Moses, 'Send some men to explore the land of Canaan, which I am giving to the Israelites. From each ancestral tribe send one of its leaders.'"

This seems like a contradiction from the Deuteronomy passage. In the Numbers passage, it appears that the Lord is giving the instructions to Moses to send spies into the land as noted above in Numbers 13:1. In Deuteronomy 1:22–23, it appears that the tribal leaders came to Moses and suggested the idea of the spies, which Moses thought to be a good idea.

I believe the motivation for the spies came from the leaders, and as Moses sought the Lord, he received God's "permissive will" to allow the spies to proceed for forty days and to bring back a report. Why do I believe this to be the case? Because God is omniscient, and He knew what was going to happen and; therefore, He used this exercise as a test of Israel's faith.

Due diligence is not always neutral in its approach to truth. Our human nature, with its hopes and fears, can manipulate our perceptions based on our will and emotions. Two years in the desert is a small amount of time to develop a genuine relationship with the living God, especially when their behaviour was full of resistance and complaint toward Moses, and by extension, toward God. Within the first two years of Moses's leadership, they expressed their desire to be back in Egypt, complained about the lack of water, and even created their own god in the form of a golden calf. God told Moses that He was ready to abandon

Diagram 12.1: - Faith vs. Fear
Numbers 13 & 14

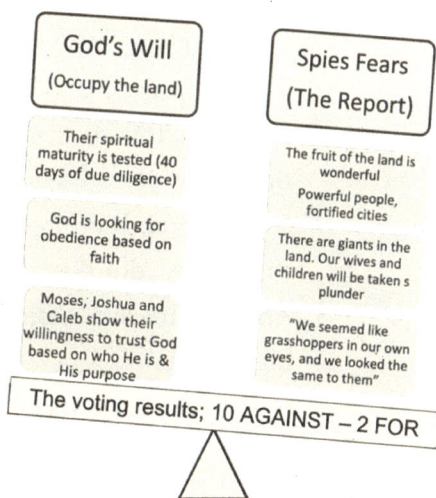

God's Will
(Occupy the land)

Spies Fears
(The Report)

Their spiritual maturity is tested (40 days of due diligence)

The fruit of the land is wonderful

Powerful people, fortified cities

God is looking for obedience based on faith

There are giants in the land. Our wives and children will be taken s plunder

Moses, Joshua and Caleb show their willingness to trust God based on who He is & His purpose

"We seemed like grasshoppers in our own eyes, and we looked the same to them"

The voting results; 10 AGAINST – 2 FOR

this group and start over again through him. It was only through Moses's intercession for God's people that God seemed to change His mind and carry on with these people.

So, based on their level of faith, their lack of commitment to God's purpose, and their lack of courage to believe that God could use them to defeat the enemy, the final report could have been written before they left to spy out the land. God knew this, and Moses should have known, based on his discernment of their spiritual maturity, but the process proceeded for the following forty days.

Lessons Learned: The bottom line is the leadership of the Israeli tribes were not ready to take the Land.

- There were only three people who expressed that the Land was ready to be taken. They were Moses, Joshua, and Caleb. These three had a strong relationship with the Lord, and their faith was strong enough to believe that God would fight for them in defeating the enemy. In Exodus 17, a victory for the Israelites in battle is described when the Amalekites attacked the Israelites and the Amalekites were defeated by the intervention of the Lord through Moses's intercession and Joshua's bravery.

- Due diligence is often based on our perceptions, which is a function of our personality.

  - The P approach is to look at things from an "is" approach. It is an analysis of what is happening right now.
  - An E approach is often based on what we "want" or, conversely, "don't want."
  - An A approach is based on "should," meaning "cost for value."
  - An I approach is based on "what does everyone else want?"

- How we see ourselves is often the way others will see us. Confidence or lack of confidence plays a significant role in leadership. We need to know what our confidence is based on and whether it has a firm foundation.

- Our faith is based on obedience to who or what we put our trust in. Are we being obedient to God, to ourselves, our abilities, or possibly to others? This is a serious problem today because we really don't know who or what to trust. The Bible tells us that God is the same yesterday, today, and forever—He can be trusted.

- Partnerships are based on the discernment of motive both in yourself and those with whom you partner. This includes the team that you lead.

- A partnership should be evaluated based on common interests and values. Does it move you closer to fulfill your purpose, assuming you know what your purpose is?

- When a group of people are unwilling to change and are more interested in perceived security than moving forward, the results can be disastrous. Throughout the forty years, many of the Israelites demonstrated a spirit of bitterness which Hebrews 12:15 says, "See to it that no one falls short of the grace of God and that no bitter root grows up to cause trouble and defile many." Bitterness can seriously impact the culture of any system and it must be dealt with as soon as it is discovered.

- Moving forward is not based on a majority vote. It is based on leadership's ability to change the culture from an A focus to an E focus.

- If our current generation cannot fulfill our purpose, then it is critical that you focus on the development of next generation leaders because you will not live forever.

The cost to the Israelites, especially those over twenty years of age, was not just the thirty-eight extra years wandering in the desert, but it also cost their lives and the special relationship that they had with God as expressed following Moses's intercession on their behalf:

> The Lord said to Moses and Aaron: "How long will this wicked community grumble against me? I have heard the complaints of these grumbling Israelites. So, tell them, 'As surely as I live, declares the Lord, I will do to you the very thing I heard you say: In this wilderness your bodies will fall—every one of you twenty years old or more who was counted in the census and who has grumbled against me. Not one of you will enter the land I swore with uplifted hand to make your home, except Caleb, son of Jephunneh and Joshua, son of Nun. As for your children that you said would be taken as plunder, I will bring them in to enjoy the land you have rejected. But as for you, your bodies will fall in this wilderness. Your children will be shepherds here for forty years, suffering for your unfaithfulness, until the last of your bodies lies in the wilderness. For forty years—one year for each of the forty days you explored the land—you will suffer for your sins and know what it is like to have me against you.' I, the Lord, have spoken, and I will surely do these things to this whole wicked community, which has banded together against me. They will meet their end in this wilderness; here they will die (Num. 14:26–35).

This is an example of a lost generation. In many ways, I believe we are experiencing the same symptoms today.

We are living among a lost generation searching for meaning in a world of turmoil. Many in our generation have no worthwhile purpose, and their values vary with time. They have no fixed position to hang on to, are motivated by fear more than anything else, and the only things that are seen as values are based on self-interest. This happens when people lose sight of God.

But God has not lost sight of them. As Christians, God's purpose for leaving us here on earth is to be His ambassadors and share a life of freedom with people who are seeking for something that they do not know what it is until we introduce them to Jesus Christ. God offers them a life of freedom through His forgiveness, and so much more. He also gives them access to His wisdom, which, as Chuck Swindoll says, offers a resource that gives us balance, strength, and insight and allows people to see circumstances from God's perspective rather than their own.

As in the case of the Exodus, God did not fail in his attempt to get the attention of His people, but the barrier of unbelief was too high to overcome. When they heard God's judgement that they would die in the desert and not enter the Promised Land, they tried to make amends by marching against the enemy. It was too late, and they were soundly defeated because they were operating in their own strength and not with the blessing of the Lord.

It is not too late for our generation, but as Christians, we must regain a sense of purpose that includes sharing the life-changing message of the Gospel with people when God gives us the opportunity. We must also trust the Holy Spirit to convict people of their neglect of

God because His Spirit is the only One who can convince people of His reality.

Are you up to the challenge? God can use you to make a difference in a lost world.

CHAPTER 13:

A Christian Leader's Lifestyle

For the past ten years, I have focused on management and leadership principles as expressed in the Bible, God's Word. One of the reasons we live in a lost generation is because we have not only lost our way in life, but we have also lost the ability to live our lives according to the foundational values that guide us along life's path. Both our purpose and our values can be found in Scripture. In Chapter Eleven, I shared the significance of the self-discipline required in order to live according to the Lord's standards.

I have learned a lot about fundamental management principles from my involvement with the Adizes Organization and its founder, Dr. Ichak Adizes. At a meeting several years ago, Dr. Adizes was sitting next to me, sharing the experience of being on a webcast with several university presidents from US institutions. He shared with us that what came out of his mouth were profound principles, and he said he had no idea where they came from.

I looked at Dr. Adizes and said, "I know where they come from." "You do?" he asked. "Yes, they come from God." I went on to tell him that in many ways he is like the prophets of the Old Testament who were challenged to speak God's truth, often to societies, even nations, who had walked away from their relationship with God. Dr. Adizes has ability to manage change on the fly based on his perception of what is going on around him and an insightful perspective based on his experience and wisdom.

I share this illustration to emphasize the need to have what Adizes calls the "gamer's mindset." Have you ever watched people when they are playing video games? They are waiting for the unexpected to happen that will cause them to lose the battle or a segment of it. It is the same in leadership; we never quite know what is going to happen next, but our followers expect us to know what to do.

In many ways, preparation and planning is the key to leadership. For some, that comes through academic or technical training and for others, it comes through experience, or both. I believe preparation is helpful, but life is filled with the unexpected. When things don't go as planned, as leaders, we are expected to deal with it.

Our preparation for the Christian life must be ongoing. We have so much to learn from God, who is more than willing to teach us, but our relationship with Him must be full time and focused.

Being a Christian leader and influencer is not a part-time experience, as God expects you to represent Him in every circumstance of your life. In the illustration of meeting with Dr. Adizes that I described earlier, I had no idea that he would be sitting next to me and talking about the webinar or what I would say to him as an encouragement. Only God knows these things, and it is God who controls our circumstances, and we must be ready for the unexpected. This readiness comes from our daily walk with Him, and it is a function of self-discipline.

We are born with the foundations of our personality, but not with character or habits. Our walk with God has a big part to play in the development of both because He is asking us to take on His character and form His habits. This requires discipline that forms habits empowered by God Himself.

As we have looked at several incidents from the life of Moses, we have seen a growing maturity in his relationship with God, which is described in Exodus 33:11: "The Lord would speak to Moses, face to face, as one speaks to a friend." This was not a once-in-a-lifetime experience for Moses; rather, this relationship occurred on a regular basis. Moses learned to turn to God for wisdom every time he faced a difficult challenge. The life of a Christian leader, to be effective, must operate the same way.

Why is this so difficult? In the early part of Moses's life, he depended so much on his own abilities, in fact, in Egypt, he was trained to depend on the strengths of his personality, which were highlighted by the ability to respond quickly to any situation with which he was confronted. Killing the Egyptian forced him to flee into the desert, and for forty years he had to learn what it meant to abide rather than act. Moses had to learn to "be" rather than "do."

> When we are born into this world, we bring two things with us, a personality shaped by God (Psalm 139) and an old nature (sin nature) that was inherited from Adam. "Therefore, just as sin entered the world through one man, and death through sin, and in this way, death came to all people, because all sinned" (Romans 5:12)

The combination of our personality and our sin nature are powerful forces that combine to do things "my way." Most of the training we receive in life, before we become Christians, is designed to support and enhance our old nature thinking with its focus on personal fulfillment and self-pride.

As a result of our belief in Jesus Christ and His sacrifice for our sin on the Cross, it was made possible for us to be forgiven, which dealt with the inherited nature of sin that we were all born with. In its place, we received a new nature, the Spirit of Jesus Christ, who came to dwell within us. Thus, our bodies became the temple of God.

What was not removed from us was the old nature, and as a born-again Christian, we have within us a battle between the old nature and the new.

The Spirit of Christ came with assets far more powerful than those that came with the old nature. For one thing, His Spirit gave us access to the Spirit of Christ and the fruit that is produced through His Spirit, which I described in Chapter Eleven. In addition, we have access to the mind of Christ, and He is committed to teaching us the meaning of truth. Truth comes in several forms, and not just right versus wrong. Truth also comes in the form of wisdom, discernment, insight, and intuition, as described in Chapter Eight.

The ultimate goal of the Christian life is not just to prepare us for eternity with God, but also to allow us to become like Jesus Himself. Jesus represents a holy life and this is what He want us to experience, as it says in 1 Peter 1:15–16: "But just as he who called you is holy, so be holy in all you do; for it is written: "Be holy, because I am holy.""

This is why we have the Spirit within us as well as the mind of Christ so that we will depend on His character and way of thinking rather than ours. One of the goals I set for myself in life is to develop as much of the fullness of His character before I depart this earth.

With such a valuable asset available to us in life and leadership, why would we ever trust ourselves more than the King of Kings and Lord of Lords?

Think about the things we deal with when we have a leadership position:

- Purpose and direction for the organization

- Decision-making, planning, and succession

- Communication with employees and teambuilding

- Development of future leadership

- Training people to handle responsibility and authority as well as accountability

- Managing conflict

- Dealing with the unexpected

- Financial challenges, cash flow, securing capital

- Developing a positive culture with defined values

- Defining and measuring success. Meeting expected results.

- Recruiting people who will have our common interest in the organization

- Putting the right people in the right roles

This is why I appreciate so much a study that focuses on the life journey of Moses. He went through the same experiences that we do every step of the way, until he let his frustration get the better of him, and he talked to God about most of them.

In order for this type of lifestyle to be real for us, we must disciple ourselves to get to know God in an intimate way. Many Christians only talk to God when either they or people close to them get into some kind of trouble. This is a "fire escape faith," and I don't believe God is impressed, but He does love you regardless. He not only wants a relationship with you but close fellowship as well. You can ask Him anything and He will answer you either through His Spirit or His Word, or both.

The older I get, the more I understand how significant my fellowship with God defines my life. I want His character to define my character, and it is not always that way because my old nature gets in the way and I can get impatient with people, especially the people I love.

God deals with me through my conscience, and I am forced to confess to Him and to the person that I have offended.

1 John 1:9 then becomes very meaningful to me: "If we confess our sins, he is faithful and just and will forgive us our sins and purify us from all unrighteousness."

I urge you not to overestimate your own abilities. Use your fellowship with God as a sounding board for the decisions you make. This requires humility on our part, and for some, that is a big problem. Leadership is about trust, which always has a two-way impact. Real trust is based on humility. Humility allows us to think about the other person more than we think about ourselves.

Trusting God is a full-time job. He wants all of you all the time. He promises to give us greater credibility because it is based on His credibility.

There is an alternative approach which I shared with you in Chapter Eight, and I do so again (emphasis mine):

> Those who let themselves be controlled by their lower natures live only to please themselves, but those who follow after the Holy Spirit find themselves doing those things that please God. Following after the Holy Spirit leads to life and peace, **but following after the old nature leads to death because the old sinful nature within us is against God. It never did obey God's laws and it never will**. That's why those who are still under the control of their old sinful selves, bent on following their old evil desires, can never please God (*LB*, Rom. 8:5–8).

CHAPTER 14:

Leadership in Action

IN HEBREWS 12:1-3, WE ARE GIVEN SOME sound advice as to how to live our lives in the same manner as the faith walk of the people described in the previous chapter, Hebrews 11:

> Therefore, since we are surrounded by such a great cloud of witnesses, let us throw off everything that hinders and the sin that so easily entangles. And let us run with perseverance the race marked out for us, fixing our eyes on Jesus, the pioneer and perfecter of faith. For the joy set before him he endured the cross, scorning its shame, and sat down at the right hand of the throne of God. Consider him who endured such opposition from sinners, so that you will not grow weary and lose heart.

There are several things in these three verses that will help us to establish a pattern to live by for the rest of our lives.

- We need to evaluate our lives and determine what is holding us back from becoming all that God wants us to be. This can be anything from our pride to our personality. What are the priorities that we hold to that are not God honouring? Ask yourself, "Do my character qualities represent the old nature within me or the new nature I received when I became a Christian? How do I treat people? Do I use people through manipulation, or do I add value to people based on their best interests?"

- We are to bring the things in our lives that are not God honouring and confess them before the Lord and ask for His forgiveness. True forgiveness results in a change in direction for us, meaning we don't go back to repeating what we have just confessed.

- Is our purpose in life marked out for us? Has God already gone ahead and marked out the trail for us to follow? The answer is yes! He has, but it looks different from the way we will tend to perceive it. The trail marked out for each of us as Christians is a relational trail, which means a life totally committed to Him, resulting in a journey of fellowship with a living God. This is what Moses understood clearly in the last forty years of his life and regardless of the challenges he faced, he would say as we should say, the joy is in the journey as God directs our circumstances.

- We must persevere in our relationship with God. This is not a one-time worship experience, but a 24/7 dynamic relationship. Discipline is essential to keep our eyes focused on the Lord because we are too easily distracted by the things that surround us and the messages within us that tell us we might be taking our faith too seriously. Part of the problem is our perception of God. We don't always see ourselves as a child of God or a friend of Jesus. Maybe we don't know Him well enough to be able to "delight yourself in the Lord, and he will give you the desires of your heart" (Ps. 37:4). God is committed to a father-child relationship and like any earthly relationship, it takes energy to keep it meaningful.

- This passage also tells us not to lose heart in our relationship with God. I believe the reason we lose heart and become weary is we so easily try to do the things that God has promised that He will take care of if we come to Him (Matthew 11:28–30).

The point of all this is to see your purpose as a relationship and not just fulfilling a particular goal. God's intention is not just to help us reach a certain target in our journey, but to prepare us and develop us for our life with Him in eternity.

How do we know what we are supposed to do in our lives if the only goal is a dynamic fellowship with God, and to enjoy the journey with Him? This is where faith comes into the picture.

From childhood, Moses understood from his parents that he was special, and God had saved him from a certain death in order to fulfill a purpose—that purpose, they believed, was to lead the Israelites from Egypt to the Promised Land as prophesied in Scripture hundreds of years prior to Moses's birth. Is it possible for God to arrange circumstances in your life to allow you to discover how you might serve Him in the most effective way possible as part of the journey you will enjoy together?

In Matthew 6:33 we are told, "But seek first his kingdom and his righteousness, and all these things will be given to you as well."

What are all these things? Matthew 6:25–32 explains what they are:

> Therefore, I tell you, do not worry about your life, what you will eat or drink; or about your body, what you will wear. Is not life more than food, and the body more than clothes? Look at the birds of the air; they do not sow or reap or store away in barns, and yet your heavenly Father feeds them. Are you not much more

valuable than they? Can any one of you by worrying add a single hour to your life?

And why do you worry about clothes? See how the flowers of the field grow. They do not labor or spin. Yet I tell you that not even Solomon in all his splendor was dressed like one of these. If that is how God clothes the grass of the field, which is here today and tomorrow is thrown into the fire, will he not much more clothe you—you of little faith? So do not worry, saying, "What shall we eat?" or "What shall we drink?" or "What shall we wear?"

Evaluate a normal day in your life. How much time do you spend worrying about everything? Past decisions, future actions, how the family is doing, health issues, inflation and the cost of things, the presentation you have to give tomorrow, the doctor's appointment next week, and on and on. We spend a lot of time worrying, which really takes our energy away from seeking God and trusting Him with every circumstance in our lives. The foundation of that relationship must be based on a two-way trust between God and ourselves.

Seeking God's Kingdom allows us to comprehend, as much as our minds will allow, the nature of God who lives within each of us when we become Christians. We will never understand it all until we are with Jesus in heaven, and even then, our learning curve will be steep. God takes us one step at a time and surfaces only those things we must act upon in obedience to Him. We are never left alone, as He is with us to handle the challenges we face. Our journey with Him always begins with Him saying to us, "Let Me take care of that!"

CHAPTER 15:

The Spontaneous Impact
of Discipline

Deciding to Let God into Your Daily
Life Creates Spontaneity.

THE MORE QUESTIONS YOU HAVE OF GOD the less likely you will be to trust Him. What I am saying is, we need to let go and let God.

Think about the most trusting relationship you have with a person, whether that be with your spouse or a lifelong friend or whomever. How often do you question their decisions or their actions? If the relationship is really based on trust, you don't ask questions because trust means that you believe the person you trust has your best interests in mind and heart. It is the same with God. He has our best interests in heart and mind. Once we realize that, we will begin to enjoy our relationship with Him and stop asking "why?"

In order for us to begin to hear Him speak, we need to discipline our schedule to spend time with Him by getting into His Word. His Spirit will speak to our spirit and our prayer times begin with, *"Abba, Father, thank You for forgiving me when I quickly go my own way, and thank You for joining me today in everything that I am doing, and thank You for the wisdom that I will receive from You today. I trust you with whatever circumstances I am faced with today."*

We are not focused on asking the "why" questions, rather, we are enjoying the relationship with Him based on mutual trust.

Understand the Power of Mutual Trust and Respect.[16]

In the Adizes methodology, the foundational philosophy for the development of a positive culture in any organization is based on mutual trust and respect for and with others. In one of his sessions, I recall Dr. Adizes saying; "Look around you. Everything you see is designed to serve something else. The desk is designed to place something on, the chair is for you to sit on, the lamp is to allow you to see more clearly." His point in this demonstration is to illustrate the principle of service to others, which begins with a foundation of humility and is demonstrated when we treat others with respect.

The Adizes definition of respect that we use in our seminars is quite simple yet profound. "Respect is demonstrated when you allow someone to think differently than you do." As associates, we add, "You don't have to agree with them, but you do have to listen to them!" This gives our human nature some comfort, but the intention of allowing someone to think differently from you is that you may learn something from that person's perspective. **Do you realize how powerful this is in management and leadership?**

It allows another person to participate in the discussion or in the decision that you are making, and for them that is a reward. For you, your tendency is to make decisions based on your default personality, which is often biased, because it doesn't consider the issues that are not your strengths. Team building is based on strengths and weaknesses working together to accomplish a task. It is based on mutual trust and respect.

What is the Adizes definition of trust? The simple definition is, "Trust exists when you believe the other person will act to protect your interests." In some ways, this sounds like a selfish purpose, but when we add the second part of the definition, its full meaning is verified. "Trust means that you take into account the interests of other people because in the long run, they are equal to your own, and that you expect the same thoughtfulness from others." What is the result of trust that is so powerful? "Trust is created when people have faith that they will benefit in the long run from their short-run sacrifices. **Employees/volunteers have a common interest in the well-being of the organization.**"[17] [20]

As there are rewards for demonstrating respect, there are also rewards for the people involved in the organization because a culture of trust between employees and management means employees will take full responsibility for their role since the success of the organization depends on ownership of their tasks. A foundational principle of managing through the development of a complementary team is that respect between people is granted freely, then trust can be demanded as part of the culture, and this becomes one of the organizations greatest assets.

Diagram 15:1- The Influence of a Leader – A Person of Integrity

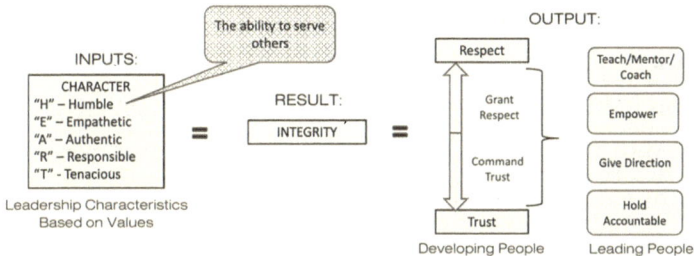

Character is learned and put into practice over the course of a lifetime and, you never stop learning if you are open and teachable

The key to creating this culture begins with the management team within the organization, and from a Christian perspective, it is a function of your character. I will borrow from John Maxwell's idea of a "Trust Test":[18(21)]

He writes, "People today are desperate for leaders, but they want to be influenced by someone they can trust, a person of good character. If you want to become someone who can positively influence other people ...

1. Model consistency of character (integrity)

2. Engage in honest communication (what you say and what you do match)

3. Value transparency (Admit your weaknesses—you are not perfect)

4. Demonstrate humility (You will lose trust with people if you demonstrate that you are driven by ego, jealousy, or the belief that you are better than they are)

5. Demonstrate support for others (Put others first—add value to others)

6. Fulfill your promises (Breaking your promises is the fastest way to break trust)."

A management team that demonstrates mutual trust and respect for each other will have a profound impact on the rest of the employees, who tend to model the accepted culture. The development of a positive culture must be supported by senior management in order to multiply that culture throughout the ranks.

That support is strengthened when authority is distributed downward so that division leaders are given the authority to make "yes" and "no" decisions for their areas of responsibility.

In order for the positive culture to grow, the division managers must be equipped and willing to utilize the strength of their team to solve problems and seek new opportunities for change. This downward thrust of decision-making is an output made possible through a positive culture of mutual trust and respect and the skillset required for the job.

The foundational philosophy of mutual trust and respect is based on a biblical principle found first in Deuteronomy 6:5, "Love the Lord your God with all your heart and with all your soul and with all your strength."

This passage was written toward the end of Moses's life, and he is recounting the key principles of his walk with the Lord as found in God's Law.

In Matthew 22:37–40, Jesus is responding to a question by a Pharisee who asked, "Teacher, which is the greatest commandment in the Law?" Jesus responds with a two-part answer:

> Jesus replied: "'Love the Lord your God with all your heart and with all your soul and with all your mind. This is the first and greatest commandment. And the second is like it: 'Love your neighbor as yourself.' All the Law and the Prophets hang on these two commandments."

Loving your neighbour as yourself is also found in Moses's writings in Leviticus 19:18. These commands are the foundation of mutual trust and respect because they are the foundation of developing trust with people. These principles were the foundation of Moses's success in leading others, and Jesus is saying that they are the foundation of your leadership today.

Do these principles of mutual trust and respect operate when working with people who do not have a strong, functional relationship with God? From my experience, the answer is yes, but it depends on where the motivation comes from in order to develop the culture of mutual trust and respect.

When I work as an Adizes associate, I teach a series of rules that are designed to establish a culture of mutual trust and respect, and I will describe those rules in the following paragraphs. The resulting culture is only sustainable as people are reminded of the rules. The problem is that human nature easily becomes the default way of behaving, which tends to revert to everyone trying to talk at the same time and can result in anything but mutual trust and respect.

God's approach is actually quite simple, as found in Deuteronomy 6:6: "These commandments that I give you today are to be on your hearts."

When they are on our hearts, these commands become part of who we are, they become part of our character, and they become part of how we live our lives. When this is true, then mutual trust and respect is sustainable in our relationships with the people we come in contact with on a daily basis.

In 2015, as an Adizes associate working with a senior associate, I had the opportunity to see mutual trust and respect at work with a hospital of five thousand employees and a budget to match. One hundred of the employees were asked to attend a two-day diagnostic to determine what needs could be identified that were causing the hospital to operate at less than its full potential. The employees were divided into three groups and asked to attend a diagnostic session, each lasting two days. The thirty-five or so people in each group represented five different layers of responsibility within the organization, from the "C" Suite executives to the people responsible for preparing the rooms for the next patient.

The two-day sessions were led by an Adizes integrator who created an environment of mutual trust and respect through a series of simple but profound rules that allowed each participant to share their perspective when it was their turn to do so. No sidebar conversations, no cellphones ringing in the meeting, no getting up to leave in order to answer a call, no speaking over one another, speak only in a defined order, and everyone pay attention to the person who is given the right to speak. It was amazing to watch as people with very different personality styles were given the freedom to share their perspective.

This culture of mutual trust and respect is how an Adizes diagnostic exercise is able to achieve the results that it does because the information for change comes from the employees themselves. This is a truly empowering exercise, especially within organizations that have a top-down culture rather than a complementary team culture.

When the information was analyzed and solutions recommended, small teams of employees from each division were asked to come up with an implementation plan using the same rules of engagement that were used during the diagnostics. Some teams came up with considerable cost-saving measures, while others discovered how to develop opportunities that were currently being missed. The overall impact through this empowering process was an increased level of energy and ownership being applied to the well-being of the hospital, increased levels of respect for one another, and ultimately an overall enhancement of a positive culture, which is what we were asked to do in the first place.

In Chapter Two, I shared a description of each of the four management styles of people whose dominant way of behaving is either P, A, E, or I. Many people have two dominant letters, sometimes three, in their style, so you may be a combination of these letters. The decision-making process that is so often required when running any organization necessitates a perspective from all four styles in order to make a good decision. The point is that you may learn a key point in making the decision that is different from your style that you hadn't thought about previously. Diagram 15.1 illustrates which styles are able to contribute to the five imperatives for making decisions.

Mutual trust and respect play a large role in decision-making, especially among division leaders and management teams. Decisions are made in the best interests of the organization, which requires trust, and effectively listening to another person's perspective requires respect.

You will note that the decision-making process should aways begin with "why you are making this decision, which often comes from the entrepreneurial perspective, but it could come from any of the styles of management if they see that change is required.

Diagram 15.2: - Decision Making; The Five Imperatives

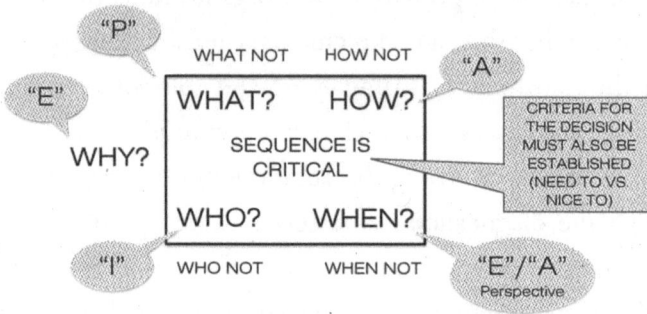

Please note the traditional sequence of "what" you are going to do, then "how" are you going to do it, followed by "when" it needs to be done, and then "who" is responsible can change. If, for example, the organization is dealing with an emergency, the sequence is then driven by "when," followed by "what," then "how," and finally "who" is responsible. The "why" in this situation is assumed as a result of the nature of the problem.

The decision-making process is also defined by the limitations of the scope of the decision, which determines the boundaries of what the decision is meant to accomplish versus what it is not required to do.

In the Adizes methodology, before you get into the details of the five imperatives, you not only need to discuss the scope of the decision, but also have a "need to" and "nice to" discussion, which addresses what must be done (need to) versus what would be nice to include but not necessary for a good decision to be made.

One more thing to think about when you take into account the different perspectives of the four management styles: The determination of "when" the decision should be made has different perspectives. Big P's and E's would want it done within twenty-four hours, while the big A's, focusing on "how" it will be done and all the details required, are reflecting on a much longer period of time. Big P's and E's need to make adjustments for reality timing based on the input from the A's and the I's, who deal with the detail, as well as who is available to take on the responsibility.

All of these things together require a working culture of mutual trust and respect.

Wherever and whenever you have the opportunity to influence others, you are leading through your influence. This is not just defined by position, your role in life, the amount of authority you have, or your ability to communicate effectively. It is defined by how you view people, whether that be in a classroom, a business, or at home with your family. Philippians 2:3–5 gives us guidelines on how we should see others, "Don't be selfish; don't try to impress others. Be humble, thinking of others as better than yourselves. Don't look out only for your own interests, but take an interest in others, too." Do you see potential in people that they have not yet discovered? Do you see people who desire to make a difference but don't quite know how? If you see yourself as helping and encouraging them in any way, then you are demonstrating a servant heart, and that is the focal point of influence.

I shared in Chapter Three, "The Foundation of Leadership," that when people were asked who the most influential person in their lives was when growing up, the majority answered their mother or grandmother. Mothers and grandmothers have a built in I, Integrator personality that they were either born with or they developed as soon as their responsibility included the well-being of a child. When mothers express a tender heart toward a child, they are actually demonstrating the character of Jesus and His care and love for us.

Love is a powerful form of leadership development, and for men it doesn't come as naturally as it does for women. Why? Why do we tend to trip over ourselves when it comes to expressing love? I believe part of the answer is that we are confused as to what love really is. True love is defined through our commitment to someone else.

There are three ways that are used in the Bible that we translate as the English word "love." They are friendship, sexual desire, and God's love. The one we are inundated with through advertising, movies, and television is sexual desire, which is devoid of the idea of commitment. The foundation of friendship and God's love for us are also both expressions of commitment. Being committed to developing a relationship with someone else takes energy and time. Loving your spouse is based on commitment. Being a parent and raising a family takes an immense amount of energy, time, and commitment. Working with a team of people in your business and developing them takes commitment. Seeing success in the students in your classroom takes commitment. Doing anything worthwhile in developing people takes commitment.

To commit yourself to another person or group of people takes not only time but also courage. As soon as you engage in leading others, you take on the responsibility to not only lead them in the right direction, but you are also responsible to develop those people with the maturity and skills required to shape the future for themselves and the roles they perform. Whenever I have been given the opportunity to lead others, I have always gone through a period of apprehension as to whether I was qualified to fulfill the responsibilities required.

In the "Adjusting" phase of my life that I shared in Chapter Ten and illustrated in Diagram 10:1, I was given an opportunity to become a chief of staff for a cabinet minister in the federal government in Canada. I wanted to do it, but I felt guilty leaving the ministry that my wife and I had led together for seven years at the Christian Embassy in Ottawa.

I sought the wisdom of the Lord in a new way, and through it, my relationship with God became much more intimate. I sensed His love for me, and I realized that He knew more about me than I knew about myself. He wanted to use the government experience to take me to a new level of purpose that required increased confidence in working with people of influence.

That move took more internal courage than becoming a teacher, and even more courage than joining a Christian ministry. But why? There were two reasons: internal doubts about myself that I could do the job, and the external opposition I felt from Christian friends and ministry associates who tried to tell me I was out of God's will! I was faced with conflicting emotions. I wanted to do it; I wasn't sure I could; and people thought I was crazy. The only person I could turn to was the Lord.

The learning curve was significant, but I enjoyed the opportunity as much as anything I have done. God was available every minute of the day to give wisdom, and the team I worked with were an inspiration through their dedication and passion to serve the minister, and through him, the government. They were a tremendous example of a complementary team.

What does it take to be willing to demonstrate commitment? Part of the answer is how you see yourself. Let's reflect on the second part of Jesus's most important commandment, "Love your neighbour as you love yourself."

The significance of the second command is based on the first. What does it take to love yourself? It means that you are satisfied with the way God made you and know that He has forgiven you and is prepared to walk with you because He loves you.

In other words, you are comfortable in your own skin! You are experiencing the freedom of Christ to be the person that God made you to be. There is no guilt in you because all the past mistakes have been taken care of between you and the Lord and between you and any other person that you may have offended. You have nothing to hide, you are not trying to be someone else, and you are free to be vulnerable with others—the real you. I often tell people that it takes a lot more energy trying to be someone else than it takes to be you.

If all of this is true, you have passed the first self-evaluation in your assessment of whether you are qualified to lead others. The next test will be a self-assessment of your willingness to respect people who are different from you in their beliefs and values, or even in the way they look and dress.

If there is anything in our lives that constrains us in being free to meet with people who are different from us, then I would suggest we need to look at ourselves and ask God to help us see people the way Jesus sees them. He sees humankind through the eyes of love.

The impact of the life of freedom is the ability to build trust with people. Relationships are really built on trust, which must start with respect. It starts with respecting a person as a human who faces all the same issues that I face at one time or another in life.

One thing I have learned about building trust is the ability to be vulnerable with others. This is the outcome of experiencing freedom. For myself, what you see is what you get, but it wasn't always that way.

Like many, my initial tendency was to protect myself from getting hurt in relationships. This was true right after my dad died when I was fourteen. I was hurt by his passing. I blamed God for taking him from me while, at the same time, I protected myself from people who tried to help me work through it. Eventually, I was able to accept the relationships of people who offered encouragement. In order to be vulnerable with people, I have to share my experiences and the impact that these have had on my life as it relates to the person who I am building trust with.

I use an illustration of being an amateur hockey goalie. I enjoyed playing this position for many years when I was younger. I explain that I would never go out on the ice without the proper equipment, especially the helmet with a cage that protected me from high-flying pucks.

I share that our initial stages of relationships are like that—we begin the relationship wearing a mask. One-on-one, both wearing masks. I decide that I am going to be the first one to take off the mask, feeling free to let the other person see the real me as the conversation proceeds.

Now the other person is the only one in the conversation who is wearing a mask, and they decide to be open and remove their mask. Trust is beginning to happen. It doesn't need to take a long period of time. I have seen it happen at a reception or a lunch meeting, and it often leads to a second opportunity to meet.

Why do I do this? I do this because I am an ambassador for Christ, and I represent Him. He came to this earth to meet the needs of people and to draw people to Himself. The Lord placed me in His diplomatic corps; He wants me to spend my time adding value to people in a hurting world. There is no greater reward for me than sharing with others the freedom that is found in a relationship with Jesus.

In the life of Moses, the courage to lead was based entirely on his relationship with God, which was not a one-time experience for him, as it shouldn't be for us. Constant change requires us to face challenging circumstances in terms of what we are trying to accomplish and with the people we are committed to leading. We need to be seeking the input of the Lord at every turn. What was it that Moses said to the fearful Israelites when they were caught in a vice between the Egyptians behind and the sea in front? **"Do not be afraid. Stand firm** and you will see the deliverance the Lord will bring you today. The Egyptians you see today you will never see again. The Lord will fight for you; you need only to be still" (Ex. 14:13–14, emphasis mine).

The Lord will give you the confidence to make the right decisions, and your credibility in leadership will come from Jesus through your relationship with Him.

CHAPTER 16:

The Courage to Confront

THE STORY OF MOSES'S LEADERSHIP WOULD NOT be complete without mentioning his ability to confront all the issues that he faced leading a group of very challenging, and quite often selfish, people for forty years.

I have previously mentioned that the default personality of the people he was leading would tend to argue, confront, and disagree with most of what Moses was saying to them. Their personality was based on the E, Entrepreneurial style of thinking that always has a better way of doing something than what was being proposed. This personality style was made even more complex through a character fault that was motivated by fear. Several times in the journey, they fought Moses in his leadership by demanding that they needed to return to the security of Egypt, even though Pharaoh was committed to keeping them in slavery. The entrepreneurial spirit can easily be subdued when our priorities focus more on security and stability than dealing head on with the challenges of change.

The thought occurs to me that when we depend entirely on our own resources in order to achieve a life of security, we end up in bondage to whomever or whatever is necessary to achieve it. Jesus has some wise words for us on this matter when dealing with people, found in Matthew 5:25, "Settle matters quickly with your adversary."

When another person has something against us or we have something against another and we don't deal with it, it will begin to eat away at us, especially if you have a high I, Integrator style in your personality. High I's will tend to avoid conflict, and that only makes the situation worse because it impacts us through pain, agony, and distress.

I can relate to this avoidance because I have a high "I," and my good friend Archie McLean, a Christian and former CEO of a large food company, taught me how to deal with it, especially if I wanted to become a more effective leader. Archie likes to use the term "constructive confrontation" when dealing with people when he is asked for advice. Basically, he is saying unless you deal with the real issues and get them on the table, it is impossible to solve the problem or address the issue effectively.

It is possible to look at conflict as a positive opportunity to make a situation better through restoration, healing, and strengthening the organizational unit in which the conflict occurs, whether that is your family, your place of employment, or elsewhere.

We have already talked about the difference in our personality and the perceptions that come from that. This can create conflict in decision-making, which can have a positive outcome if we are willing to listen to another person's viewpoint because it may be something that we needed to see and learn from.

I have witnessed poor behaviour within an organization when an employee shares their negative thoughts with others about management decisions. They often don't talk to the person they are accountable to, but they feel free to share with peers in water cooler conversations. If this is not corrected quickly, it can impact the culture within an organization, depending on how others deal with these sidebar conversations. If this behaviour does not change, then removing the person from the organization is appropriate.

Confrontation is often avoided. Why? There is risk of being rejected, fear of failure—making the situation worse by creating anger and resentment with the person confronted. **Avoiding confrontation (or talking to someone who can't solve the issue) makes the situation worse.** Confrontation is a chance to help develop people if done with respect and with the other person's interest at heart.

Much advice has been given about how to deal with conflict, and I appreciate the input of John Maxwell, who shares the following ten guidelines:[19]

1. Confront as soon as possible

2. Address the wrong action, not the person

3. Confront only what the person can change

4. Give the person the benefit of the doubt

5. Be specific

6. Avoid sarcasm

7. Avoid words like "always" and "never"

8. Where possible share your feelings about what the person did that was wrong

9. Give the person a game plan to fix the problem

10. Affirm him or her as a person and a friend

This input is most useful for to one-on-one dialogue with another person, but this is not the only source of conflict that we are confronted with.

One of the lessons learned from the study of Moses's leadership is the significance of his relationship with God in dealing with tough situations. He sought the Lord's input before he engaged in dealing with conflict. Often conflict is a manifestation of a deeper root problem that needs to be addressed before solutions can be applied. For example, in the Exodus, the people Moses was leading faced the fundamental problem of unbelief, or lack of trust in God. They did not understand that God had their best interests at heart.

The Israelites were God's chosen people through whom the Messiah would enter the world in order to deal with the foundational issue of sin and the separation from God through the power of forgiveness. All of this was to happen in the Promised Land, centuries in the future, thus it was part of God's long-term plan for the restoration of humankind to Himself. Very few of the Israelites would have understood this.

This is another type of conflict that is very common within the environments we are familiar with today. This is a long-term–short-term conflict. Most of the Israelites did not have the same faith that Moses had. They had been living in a pagan world prior to their rescue and they had taken on the values of a pagan society. They were more interested in their personal security and well-being than they were in the purposes of God. What did they complain about?

They found security in slavery. At the first sign of trouble, they told Moses that if would be far better to return to Egypt than to continue the journey! They complained on several occasions about the lack of water and food. God provided food and water for them through His promised provision that He would never leave them or forsake them, but they were looking only at their immediate needs. They wanted a different menu from the manna that God provided on a daily basis, so God provided them with meat to eat as well. The first generation of Israelites that came out of Egypt were very self-centered.

This is what happens in a society that finds a way to eliminate God from their daily lives. Sound familiar? Our society is inundated with leaders who do not consider God in the decisions that can affect so many others. There are millions of Christians in this world, but many who claim an identity with the faith do not necessarily have a vibrant relationship with God. The people who came out of Egypt saw themselves as Israelites from a cultural perspective, but they lacked a dynamic trust relationship with a living God. What Moses, Joshua, Aaron, and Caleb understood was that the reality of a close walk with God impacted every decision that they made.

What we need to understand, which I have learned from Adizes and life, is that disintegration in any system happens naturally. Because of change and the inability to handle change, the systems begin to fall apart or disintegrate, which in turn creates conflict.

I like to use the example of my human body. Before I was twenty years of age, I had to have operations on both knees as a result of sport injuries. Later in life, I struggled with acute osteoarthritis as a result of living with bone-on-bone in both knees. When I reached the age of seventy-three in 2018, I had both knees replaced with the advice of the surgeon who told me, "We want to give you your life back!"

Prior to the operations, I realized that the human body is made up of different systems and some disintegrate faster than others. I used to tell people that my birth certificate told me I was seventy-three, my head and heart (vision) felt that I was forty, but my knees felt like they were 120! The surgery and subsequent physio gave me a renewed energy and my system was reintegrated as one. This is an illustration of what is

needed to manage any system, whether that is your family, your business, or your profession. Disintegration drains energy from any system, which requires the application of energy in order to reintegrate the system.

Knowing how to reintegrate the system requires the knowledge of where the disintegration is coming from. In the Adizes presentations, we often use the picture of an iceberg to illustrate the difference between the manifestations of a problem versus the root of the problem, as shown in Diagram 16.1. The top 10% of the iceberg represents the manifestations, while the bottom 90% represent the root causes. It was the bottom 90% that ripped into the hull of the *Titanic* that caused the loss of 1,504 lives.

These conflicts include roles and responsibilities, as well as long-term versus short-term issues. Short term (PA) issues always win out because this is where we spend more than 90%of our time and energy. Long term (EI) issues are often put on the back burner, especially if the system is in the Go-Go phase of the Lifecycle.

Conflict can occur when there is a lack of clear understanding of responsibility and/or authority to make "yes" and "no" decisions. Accountability can also be a conflict producer, especially if the lines of accountability are not clear in the organizational structure. A person may be asked to report to two people because they are being asked to perform two jobs, especially in the Go-Go stage of the Lifecycle. A variance in expectations can also cause conflict when the expectations of the employer are not clearly understood by the employee and vice versa.

Differences in our personality can cause conflict in a number of ways. As explained in Chapter Two, different personalities perceive things in different ways; big P's see things from "what is happening right now," while big A's "see things from a "cost for value" perspective. Big E's look at things from a "want" perspective while big "I's" desire for unity, and as a result they try to avoid conflict. How different styles perceive reality can cause conflict in any system unless mutual respect is strongly enforced.

I have worked in organizations where making a good decision is seen as the end of a critical process only to find out that there was no plan put together to implement the decision. This not only caused conflict but also frustration, as several ongoing meetings were dedicated to the lack of progress on the good decision that was made. The conflict between decision-making and implementation is common in many organizations. Unless a specific implementation plan is developed, the decision will often remain dormant.

One of the values of the Adizes methodology is defining a common language that all can agree on. For example, when we are looking for potential improvement points in any system, are we looking for problems or opportunities? Dr. Adizes points out that change drives both opportunities and threats, so he calls them "opporthreats" based on the Chinese symbol, which is the same for both. This concept can change our thinking as to how we handle a problem. Can we turn the problem into an opportunity that will require an entrepreneurial approach to problem solving rather than a strictly administrative approach?

Having worked in government, I noticed that the default approach to problem solving is to address problems from an administrative (A) perspective. This system is designed to tackle problems through the development of new policies because most governments are administrative systems. The thing that is missing is a balanced approach that takes into account the other three roles of management, including creative new ideas, outsourcing to private enterprises who have more experience with the issue, and seeking advice from people and institutions that are experts in the field.

The way governments handle many issues create conflict based on their philosophical perspective or world view that they believe is in the best interest of the people they serve. The democratic process is designed to offer the right of dissension, which is supposed to offer a dialogue between people with opposing views. This process should create a better idea than the one initially proposed, but it seldom works because the majority opinion rules the day, as narrow as that majority may be.

Decisions are made and implemented based on the majority numbers, but often this creates conflict because many people feel their views are not heard or taken into consideration. As I heard one politician say recently, "I have never seen people in our country feel so angry." Our democratic institutions are becoming more like glorified dictatorships because mutual trust and respect is no longer having the impact that it should. Our democracies in the Western world are desperately in need of statesmen who are gifted in the process of integration because they can see value in both sides of an argument.

A critical point in the Exodus comes at Kadesh-Barnea when the Israelites were two years into the journey. In Chapter Twelve, "Being Lost Can Become a Way of Life," I explained the opportunity that God gave the Israelites to take the Promised Land and the results of what happened when they spied out the land for forty days.

Let us take a look at where the Israelites were at on the Organizational Lifecycle diagram from a PAEI role perspective. The growing phases are shown with the solid black line and the ageing phases with the broken black line. Both phases are not a function of time, rather, they are more a function of organizational maturity, or lack of it, than anything else.

The letters PAEI define the roles for each phase of the Lifecycle, and the dominant letters for each phase are shown in capital letters.

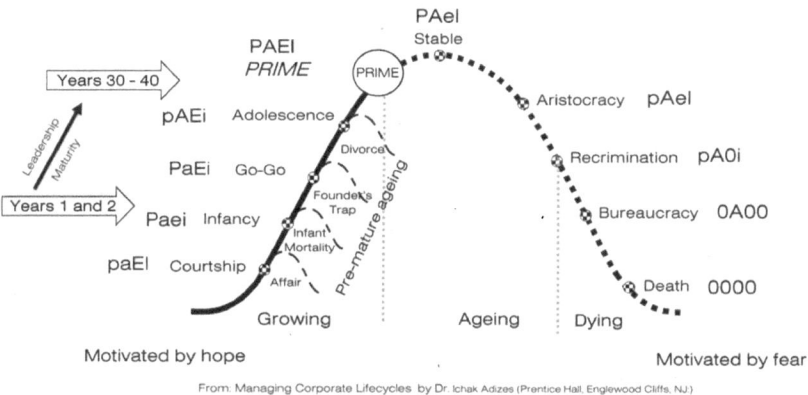

Diagram 16.2: The Lifecycle position shift during the 40 years of the Exodus

From: Managing Corporate Lifecycles by Dr. Ichak Adizes (Prentice Hall, Englewood Cliffs, NJ.)

I believe the organizational structure of the Exodus that was outlined in Exodus 18 by Jethro was the *beginning* of the administrative infrastructure development that was necessary to support a journey that required getting between 2.5 to 3 million people from Egypt to the Promised Land. This was an authority distribution structure with responsibility defined by the numbers of people each leader was responsible for: thousands, hundreds, fifties, and tens. Their responsibility was to lead and educate according to the principles of the Lord as Moses passed the instructions down. They were to organize and train the people to handle the day-to-day tasks and also learn how to defend themselves militarily. I believe by the time they arrived at Kadesh-Barnea two years later, they would have been in late Infancy or early Go-Go on the Lifecycle.

The ability to assign authority to a group of people, as Jethro's advice suggested, is only one aspect required in the development of an effective organization. The qualifications for leadership proposed by Jethro were reliable in that he suggested the men Moses chose should be "… capable men from all the people—men who fear God, trustworthy men who hate dishonest gain—and appoint them as officials over thousands, hundreds, fifties and tens" (Ex. 18:21).

Did these men *contribute* to the purpose alongside Moses as an effective management group based on trust? Did they own the *purpose* of the organization as Moses did? Had they *proven* their leadership ability within the initial first few months of the journey out of Egypt when Jethro shared his advice? Did these men have the trust of the people for whom they were responsible? Were there other men with strong influence who tried to undermine the leadership of these men and by extension undermine the leadership of Moses? The answers are unknown, but the decisions made at Kadesh-Barnea would suggest that two years was too short a time to evaluate their leadership ability, especially from a character development perspective.

Following hundreds of years in Egypt and two years under God's Law, their faith and their ability to trust God was limited. In the first two years of the journey, they certainly had not demonstrated their dependence on God or in their deep trust of Moses.

One of the key roles for leadership in any organization is to determine the capacity of the organization and its ability to deal with change. It is very easy, especially in faith-based organizations, to overestimate the ability to handle market shifts and the needs that surface as a result of change.

Many faith-based organizations rely on volunteers to do the work of the ministry, and the leadership development required to perform the work is seen only as a part-time function. This means that leadership capacity is often less than what is required to take on major shifts in expansion or changes in strategy.

As significant as faith is to the success of the organization, measuring the capacity of an organization is a management function that must be based on reality. A realistic approach to current and future capacity must be performed. Capacity measurement must take into consideration such things as:

- Leadership requirements for expansion

- Cultural changes for specific markets the organization is trying to impact

- Strategy changes required to accommodate these changes

- Physical changes; the ability to secure land for expansion would be an example

- Financial requirements and the ability to secure financial capital

- Administrative efficiency and measurement of results

- Technology changes; the recent COVID pandemic has changed the way we communicate with one another via remote rather than in-person gatherings.

- Political changes that impact directly on the organization

The Lord knew the Israelites were not ready to enter the land so this was a test of their faith, which limited their capacity to take the Promised Land. The Lord does the same thing with us through the circumstances that He brings our way. If they had an attitude and willingness to trust in God, just as Joshua and Caleb demonstrated, I believe the results would have been very different.

I believe as Christians, when God calls us to leadership positions, He will often test our faith in order to keep our relationship with Him on the front burner of our lives. He will let us know if we are ready to handle the opportunities before us. Sometimes we just need to wait for His green light that may require changes within the organization itself.

A new leadership team had to be developed in order to take the Exodus into the Promised Land. That leadership team would be comprised of next generation leaders because the first generation, defined by their unbelief and lack of trust in God, would die in the desert over the next thirty-eight years. Moses's mentoring of Joshua would, in many ways, define Moses's legacy, as it would be Joshua who would take the next generation into God's Promised Land.

Choosing the right leadership in any organization is critical for its success. It takes time to develop leaders and to watch people grow in their ability to handle authority and to determine if they "own" the enterprise as keenly as the person at the top.

Referring again to Diagram 16.2, I would like to use the Lifecycle diagram to explain the significance of the Adolescence stage. In this stage, there are many adjustments that need to be made in order to move from Go-Go to Prime.

This journey requires a move from an entrepreneurial style of management to a professional style of management. This is a difficult transition in most organizations since the entrepreneurial style is usually based on one person, the founder (or founders in some cases), who developed the dream based on his or her PAEI entrepreneurial management style. This is a visionary, risk-taking style, committed to overcoming all odds to make the organization grow.

In the early stages of Go-Go, there are not many systems designed to measure performance or return on investment. The journey through Adolescence requires the development of A, Administrative systems without losing the entrepreneurial spirit (E) within the organization.

In the Adolescence stage there is an increased role for the management team who take on greater responsibility for the success of the organization rather than depending on the founder as it was in Go-Go. The founder may still be the leader and drive the vision, but the management team takes on the responsibility to develop strategies and plans for the long term, usually eighteen months to three years, while managing the short-term and being conscious of the major outside influences that can bring about needed change in the way the organization is run. The management team must debate amongst themselves the four roles of management necessary to run the organization, regardless of what their personal management style looks like.

This is an expression of a professionally run organization. The four roles of management are institutionalized within the management team and the organizational goals (for a business) shift from revenue to profitability. Within Adolescence, a balance is developed between the flexibility to make decisions and controllability to make sure the returns on investment are worth the energy being applied. The organization is still driven by a preferred future as expressed through the E role, but with an effective consideration for the costs involved in making it happen. The Adolescence stage on the Lifecycle represents the necessary pain an enterprise must go through in order to prepare for Prime.

The problem of conflict arises when and if members of the management team default to their personal management style or they allow their management input to be motivated by their personal interests rather than the organizational interests. I believe this is what happened at Kadesh-Barnea in the Exodus journey. Leaders were motivated by fear and lack of trust, which allowed them to perceive the worst-case scenario. When they presented their report, they shared it in front of the entire assembly of Israelites instead of to Moses alone. Fear is easily multiplied in the lives of others, as is lack of trust. These consequences were judged by God as a rebellion against Him, and He made His judgements accordingly.

It would take many years for Moses to oversee the development of an effective and efficient management team. I estimate that real progress in this area was seen in the last ten years of the journey. The first generation of the Exodus would have died off based on God's judgement, and a new generation had to be trained to take their place. Moses would have involved Joshua with every decision, as we must do when we are training key people for the future. Management and leadership development principles must work hand in hand and always be driven by a renewed perspective of the vision and purpose for the organization. It was this energy that Joshua would provide for his new team of leaders and managers in order to take the Promised Land and fulfill God's calling on Moses and the Israelite people.

As close as Moses's relationship was with God (face-to-face), he had to deal with his own emotions as exhibited in his frustration, and on occasion not knowing what to do next as he was faced with the challenges of leadership. As far as I can tell, he never allowed himself to become bitter about what the Lord had called him to do because he saw himself as fulfilling God's purpose, which allowed him to remain positive to the end of his earthly journey.

There is much that we can learn from his story of faith as a leader, and in the final chapters I will try to leave you with the potential that God sees in you to become His ambassador in the journey that He wants you to take.

CHAPTER 17:

Called to Serve in Times of Change

OUR ABILITY TO LEAD WELL AND TO manage effectively is required in a world that is facing constant change. We will need a firm foundation from which we make the decisions that ultimately impact people whether that be raising our children, leading a church, serving in a profession, or running a business.

One of the defining qualities of a leader is the ability to understand the impact of change through **intuition**, which John Maxwell defines as "the ability to discern intangible factors, understand them, and work with them to accomplish leadership goals."[20] For the Christian leader, insight and discernment come from our access to the mind of Christ. It is this gift, offered by grace through the Holy Spirit, that allows us to put the pieces together to understand the winds of change and how they will impact our lives, and through us the lives of others. Adizes call this "having a gamer's mindset," which I spoke about in Chapter Thirteen.

My friend Chris Ayon, a pastor in Dallas, Texas, shared an interesting insight on a recent Zoom call when he spoke about the sinking of the *Titanic*. The *Titanic* had three classes of service: first, second, and third, called steerage. First class was found on the upper decks and was reserved for the wealthiest travellers. Third class was in the lower decks, and was reserved for the commoners. Second class was somewhere in between. When the ship hit the iceberg, it shuddered with the impact, but almost immediately, the first-class passengers went about what they were doing as if nothing had happened. The iceberg tore a large hole in the ship below the waterline. The immediate experience was quite different for people in the lower decks than those in the upper decks, with one group going about their routines as if nothing had happened, and the other fighting for their lives. Regardless of their location on the ship, the next few hours would bring a sober evaluation for each of them as they reviewed their life journey to that point.

I believe every Christian is called to lead in one way or another based on where they find themselves on life's journey, whether that is in business, the professions, at home with the family, or even in their retirement years. I encourage you to never stop evaluating where you are in your walk with the Lord and what it will take for you to reach spiritual Prime and a life of significance.

What does it take for us to evaluate who we are, and especially the quality of our relationship with God? Life is a journey, and much of this book has been devoted to the lessons learned from the life of Moses that can easily be applied to us. Moses is known as one of the greatest leaders in the Bible, so, my assumption is that we can use his learning curve (more of a roller-coaster ride than a consistent growth curve) to define what Prime looked like for him toward the end of his life and what he had to go through in order to get there. As an aside, you don't have to wait until you get to the end of your life in order to reach Prime; you can get there much earlier.

What Does Spiritual Prime Look Like?

For Christians, our leadership foundation is found in our relationship with God. To be a disciple of Jesus Christ is not a part-time job; it requires our full attention such that we can exclaim with the psalmist at the end of our lives, "I have walked in my integrity and I have trusted in the Lord without wavering" (Ps. 26:1). As Horace Greely wrote, "Fame is a vapor, popularity an accident, riches take wing, and only character endures." [24]

The Christian life is a life of purpose that is intended to line up with God's purpose in the way we live and in what we do. Life is a constant journey of maturing and not easily learned without discipline or self-control, and the ultimate outcome is a life of fulfillment based on service to others. As a friend said recently on our Bibles and Bros. call after he shared his God-centred divine appointments, "Wow, I am being used by God!"

One of the outcomes of our life of faith is the belief that God controls our circumstances, and our response to those circumstances is how we grow as a Christian. It means that we keep learning and trusting as we seek input from the Lord and deepen our relationship with Him. We must discipline ourselves to get into His Word on a regular basis, and we must learn to listen to what the Holy Spirit is telling us as we hear Him speak through the Word and the Spirit. I encourage you to write down what He is saying to you and review it as a way to measure your own spiritual maturity. Share what you learn with others, especially the principles of leadership that are so obvious and can be confirmed through your own experiences.

What does it take to continue to grow in our relationship with God and to sense that we are in our Prime? What does that mean? I have described this previously as moving from success to significance, but this is a nebulous definition if you have never defined success or what significance looks like in your life. We tend to use human definitions to define both, but what are God's definitions for success and significance? I can only give you my interpretation as it applies to my life as I look back over my seventy-nine years.

First let me illustrate how I see Moses's life journey and then compare what he went through to what I believe we often go through as leaders. Diagram 17.1 illustrates Moses's spiritual journey on the Lifecycle alongside a comparative table showing what he went through

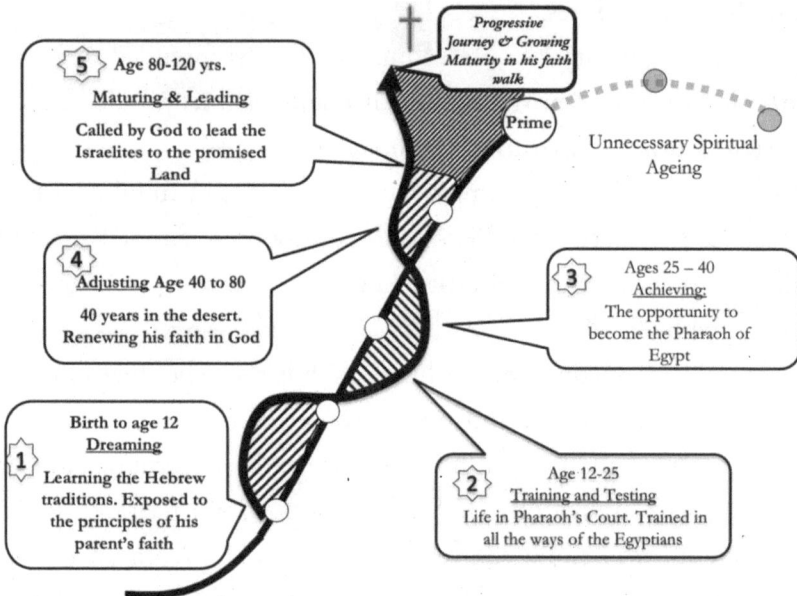

Diagram 17.1: Moses 120 Year Spiritual Growth Curve

5 Age 80-120 yrs.
Maturing & Leading
Called by God to lead the Israelites to the promised Land

Progressive Journey & Growing Maturity in his faith walk
Prime

Unnecessary Spiritual Ageing

4 Adjusting Age 40 to 80
40 years in the desert. Renewing his faith in God

3 Ages 25 – 40
Achieving:
The opportunity to become the Pharaoh of Egypt

Birth to age 12
Dreaming
1 Learning the Hebrew traditions. Exposed to the principles of his parent's faith

2 Age 12-25
Training and Testing
Life in Pharaoh's Court. Trained in all the ways of the Egyptians

at each phase and what we might expect in our journey of faith.

Lifecycle Phase	Moses's Life	My Life/Your Life
1. Dreaming	Moses's faith journey began through his parents, who taught him the faith traditions of the Hebrew people until he was nearly twelve years of age. They would have told him what they believed, and that he was destined to lead the Israelites from Egypt and take them to the Promised Land.	When God placed His hand on you and called you into His service, He place the heart of God within you, a desire to know Him more. This would result in a born-again experience for you when, through you asking for forgiveness, the fullness of the Holy Spirit would enter your life and you became a child of God. (See Romans 8:29–30 and Romans 8:14–17.)
2. Training and Testing	Around age twelve, Moses was taken into Pharaoh's household by Pharaoh's daughter to be raised as her stepson. Moses began his training in all the ways of the Egyptians to prepare him to become the next Pharaoh. A male heir had to lead Egypt following the death of Pharaoh.	In the early years of your faith journey with God, the challenge for you was to make the faith of your parents, or your upbringing, your personal faith. This is a period of testing for you and temptations may cause you to take your eyes off Jesus and your faith is weakened.

Lifecycle Phase	Moses's Life	My Life/Your Life
3. Achieving	Moses was trained as a military and administrative leader in order to lead the most powerful country in the world at that time. The Hebrew people had become slaves and he was troubled by their mistreatment to the point that he killed an Egyptian overlord. This was discovered and Moses had to escape to the desert in the Land of Midian	You learn your strengths and weaknesses through experience. You advance in your career. You will usually get married in this stage and begin to grow a family. Life becomes very hectic. You have a lot going for you and you depend on your natural strengths to solve life's problems. You don't have a lot of serious time to grow your relationship with God. A personal crisis may bring your attention back to the Lord.
4. Adjusting	From leadership preparation in Egypt to looking after sheep for forty years! This was a time for Moses to reflect on his faith as God speaks to him. He began to write the book of Genesis through God's input. He revisited his childhood vision, but he felt defeated and discouraged, even though this was the greatest learning experience of his life from a spiritual perspective—knowing God in a deeper way.	Your responsibilities begin to change and experience at work has given you greater opportunities. Your children are now young adults and their need is more for advice than direction. You may find yourself looking after your parents or in-laws as an additional challenge. You begin to think about the difference between "success" and "significance" in your faith journey and your desire is to know God in a deeper way.

Lifecycle Phase	Moses's Life	My Life/Your Life
5. Leading	Moses began to understand the foundations of godly leadership, which is based on serving others and developing them. Even though he was hesitant, he accepted God's challenge to lead the Israelites out of Egypt, which became the biggest challenge of his life. They were an obstinate people who did not know God in a personal way and they fought Moses's every decision. God stood with Moses in his leadership and Moses constantly interceded for the people he was leading because he owned the responsibility God had given him. On most occasions, Moses trusted God to handle the challenges through God's resources rather than his own. His relationship with God grew and is described in Exodus 33:11 as "God would speak to Moses face-to-face as a man speaks with his friend."	God reaffirms your vision to add value to people. This includes your family, which is now growing with the addition of grandchildren, and you see the future in them. You want to do all you can to encourage them in their faith and teach them the biblical principles that will help them handle the challenges of life after you are gone. You want to do the same for the people you work with or lead, and you want to make a difference in the lives of people who are struggling, whom God will lay on your heart. You know God will open opportunities for you through the circumstances that He controls, and you are living with the knowledge that God loves you and your family, and He will use you to glorify His name as you serve Him with the fullness of your heart and the strength He has given you.

As mentioned, Moses's faith journey began through his parents, who taught him the faith traditions of the Hebrew people until he was nearly twelve years of age. They would have told him what they believed, and that he was destined to lead the Israelites from Egypt and take them to the Promised Land.

Moses's life actually began with a heart for God that was placed in him by God Himself through the gift of His grace.

This was also true for me, although I didn't realize it until later in life. My spiritual success was realized when I understood that God was calling me to have a relationship with Him. That relationship was based on the need to be forgiven and my asking Him to forgive me. As a result, He indwelt me with His Spirit, the Holy Spirit whom He calls the "Comforter." He names me as His child, and I call Him Abba, Father. Through it all I became a citizen of heaven while on this earth but with the privileges of a future in heavenly places. This is the foundation of spiritual success, which is necessary in order to achieve a life of significance.

As my faith matured, I began to understand the meaning of significance from God's point of view. Significance is not defined by what you do in life, but rather who you are or who you will become based on your growing relationship with God. Your journey with God is more about being than doing. But out of your being, the Lord calls you to be part of His plan, which can only be accomplished through obedience to Him, and this is where the adventure becomes real.

This journey is by no means static. It is dynamic and constantly changing based on the circumstances in your life. This is a progressive journey, and it requires numerous adjustments that are required in order to keep your eyes on the Lord and not on yourself or on what the world considers success.

There is one more thing that Jesus expects from you in this growing relationship: He wants to trust you with the future. Just like in Moses's life, God not only trusted him with getting the Israelites to the

Promised Land, but He also trusted him with His long-term purposes for humankind. As mentioned previously, God's long-term plan was for the revelation of the Messiah and the salvation of humankind, a gift that would come through the lineage of the Jewish people. (See Matthew, Chapter 1)

The last words Jesus shared with His disciples prior to His ascension was a challenge to continue the ministry that they had seen demonstrated for the three-and-a-half years while they were with Him. That message was to "… go into the whole world and make disciples…" (Matt. 28:19). Christianity was meant to become a movement energized through the changed life of thousands of believers, generation after generation. The eleven disciples that heard Jesus's message were faithful to the call and empowered by the Holy Spirit. Through the process of multiplication, you and I are Christians today.

So, what is our responsibility to the next generation? God holds us responsible for the expression and demonstration of the Gospel to future generations. This is not just about sharing the message, but also living it and training others how to live it and to share it so they can pass it on to others.

Where do we begin? Again, evaluate your sphere of influence, starting with your family. Our four adult children are now in their forties and fifties, so our role is to encourage and offer advice when they ask for it and to try to build as strong an influence as possible with our eight grandchildren, who range in age from six to their early twenties. This is not a one-way relationship but, rather like most deep relationships, they are mutually beneficial.

What about your business or profession? You can have a big influence on the people you work alongside through a listening ear and the expression of encouragement. When people see you as a person of integrity, they will be far more willing to enter into a trust relationship that may give you an opportunity to add value to their lives through the expression of your values. A person with a close relationship with the Lord will be recognized as different, and, in my experience, those who are intrigued in a positive way will not be shy about asking why and how.

There is no better example for Wendy and me than our daughter Karen and the influence that she has on her students as she teaches senior mathematics at the high school level. For many years, at the end of the school term, she has received letters of appreciation from students who have been impacted by her influence and teaching. These notes bring tears to our eyes, as we see Jesus Christ living through her as a result of her commitment that goes far beyond their time in the classroom.

Diagram 17.2 illustrates our spiritual Lifecycle with the growing phases on the left and the Ageing phases on the right. This diagram is similar to the one in Chapter 10 but with more of an emphasis on the priorities required to experience a life of significance. Based on our experience, the roller-coaster black line represents our faith journey. It shows five distinct phases that impacted our lives.

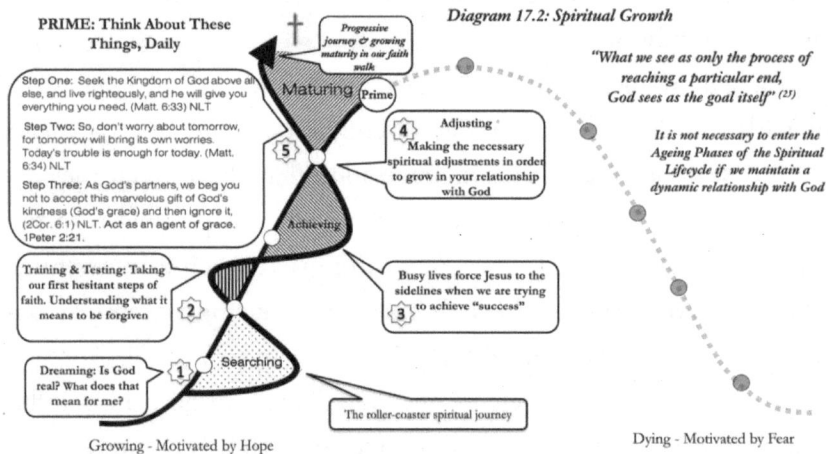

PRIME: Think About These Things, Daily

Progressive journey & growing maturity in our faith walk

Maturing (Prime)

Step One: Seek the Kingdom of God above all else, and live righteously, and he will give you everything you need. (Matt. 6:33) NLT

Step Two: So, don't worry about tomorrow, for tomorrow will bring its own worries. Today's trouble is enough for today. (Matt. 6:34) NLT

Step Three: As God's partners, we beg you not to accept this marvelous gift of God's kindness (God's grace) and then ignore it. (2Cor. 6:1) NLT. Act as an agent of grace. 1Peter 2:21.

5

Achieving

4 Adjusting
Making the necessary spiritual adjustments in order to grow in your relationship with God

Training & Testing: Taking our first hesitant steps of faith. Understanding what it means to be forgiven

2

3 Busy lives force Jesus to the sidelines when we are trying to achieve "success"

Dreaming: Is God real? What does that mean for me?

1 Searching

The roller-coaster spiritual journey

Diagram 17.2: Spiritual Growth

"What we see as only the process of reaching a particular end, God sees as the goal itself" (21)

It is not necessary to enter the Ageing Phases of the Spiritual Lifecycle if we maintain a dynamic relationship with God

Growing - Motivated by Hope

Dying - Motivated by Fear

When the roller-coaster line moves to the inside of the bell curve, these areas reflect periods of searching or premature spiritual ageing, and the characteristics are similar to institutionalized ageing on the right-hand side of the curve. The description of spiritual ageing, either premature or permanent, is illustrated in this diagram and will be discussed in the next chapter.

In the maturing phase, there are three steps that we found helpful in maintaining and growing in our relationship with God. This was a progression, a critical point of understanding in our faith journey regarding the role of the Holy Spirit in our life, and shared in Chapter Ten, but it didn't happen overnight.

Step One: "Seek the Kingdom of God above all else, and live righteously, **and he will give you everything you need**" (*NLT*, Matt. 6:33, emphasis mine).

When you were born again and experienced regeneration, new birth, then sanctification begins. The end result of sanctification (becoming like Christ) is to become holy as God is holy. You are actually a new creation, but you have to grow in your relationship with God because you don't become like Christ on the day you were born again. This potential for change was deposited within you when you asked Him to forgive you. His Spirit is the teacher.

This is unique and personal, designed specifically for you, and the training environment is provided through the circumstances that you are faced with on a daily basis. He will bring people across your path that will help you to grow in your relationship with Him. God already knows what you are going through and what you have to deal with. Why then would you try to handle all these things through your own resources? God is begging you to let Him into your life to assist with the challenges that you face.

Step Two: "So, don't worry about tomorrow, for tomorrow will bring its own worries. **Today's trouble is enough for today**" (*NLT*, Matt. 6:34, emphasis mine).

Lasting anxiety is when we worry about the circumstances for today, tomorrow, next week, and so on. Our old nature is really good at this, and it is consistently being fine-tuned. This means the more we worry about things, the more granular the worry issues become, and we start worrying about the things that we never used to. This is a function of age, experience, and fear, and it is one of the reasons that Jesus tells us to think and trust like children. We don't often see a lot of worry coming from children when they have a loving relationship with their mom and dad. Jesus wants to take our worries from us when we cast them on Him.

Anxiety can take the joy out of life, and the stress produced can kill you. I saw the impact on my dad when he had a lot of responsibility working as the manager of the jet engine division at Rolls-Royce, Canada. He would often work late evenings and also Saturdays in order to complete the work. He was responsible and driven as many big P's are, but it cost him his health, as he suffered a nervous breakdown and two heart attacks, with the last one taking his life three days before his fiftieth birthday.

We live in a culture of ever-increasing fear because we are unable to solve the problems we face. Jesus is asking us to bring every opportunity that would cause stress in our life to Him. How often? Daily!

> Come to me, all you who are weary and burdened, and
> I will give you rest. Take my yoke upon you and learn
> from me, for I am gentle and humble in heart, and you
> will find rest for your souls. For my yoke is easy and
> my burden is light (Matt. 11:28–30).

Step Three: "As God's partners, we beg you not to accept this marvelous gift of God's kindness [God's grace] and then ignore it" (*NLT*, 2 Cor. 6:1). "Act as an agent of grace" (1 Pet. 2:21).

Charles Swindoll, in his daily devotional, shares these thoughts about God's grace: "To show grace is to extend favor or kindness to one who doesn't deserve it and can never earn it. Receiving God's acceptance by grace always stands in sharp contrast to earning it on the basis of works. ... Favor is being extended simply out of the goodness of the heart of the giver."[21]

I believe that to grow in our relationship with God over the course of our life we are called to give away what God has given to us. This is the idea behind 1 Peter 2:21: "To this you were called, because Christ suffered for you, leaving you an example, that you should follow in his steps." We are to become agents of grace. But how?

Begin by evaluating your circle of influence. Close friends, family, people you work with, students in your classroom, the people who fill the pews in your church, your neighbours, the people who represent you in government, as well as the people whom God lays on your heart, which may be someone you don't know but God brings across your path today.

Now, think about the word *trust* as the foundation of influence. Ask God to help you build trust with any of the people that I have mentioned. Allow God to arrange the circumstances for you to meet them, which I would call a divine appointment, which then allows you to begin the trust relationship together.

Fifty plus years ago, when I was a high school teacher, I was known as a disciplinarian, and as such I was able to maintain an environment of control in the classroom. I had seen some teachers who tried to be the students' best friend and their classrooms were often quite chaotic. The problem with my approach was for some, it was based on fear. They were afraid to step out of line. I realized that fear does not create the best learning environment.

Early on in my career, I developed a two-prong strategy that included volunteering to coach many of the schools' extracurricular athletic activities. I used to joke about my demeanor in the class-room as, "Don't smile until Christmas." It is impossible to build trust within an environment of fear, but the coaching activities allowed me to serve students in a totally different way. I also taught many of the students that I coached, so our relationship of trust carried over to the classroom, which changed the environment, and it had a big impact in allowing the students to enjoy being in the classroom. This became the foundation of my teaching philosophy, which I have shared with others: "If students enjoy being in the classroom with you, you can teach them anything!"

One of God's principles of service to others demonstrates that when you put others first, trust is more readily established.

Connect Before Calling—The Key to Building Trust

Do you recall hearing the statement, "People don't care how much you know until they know how much you care?" This is foundational to building trust with people, and we are reminded of this truth from the beginning to the end of Jesus's servant leadership style of ministry.

Luke Chapter 5 gives us an explanation of the type of people Jesus was looking for, who would be willing to follow Him and be able to carry on His work.

He was speaking to a crowd on the shore of the Sea of Galilee, and, being pressed by the crowd, he got into a fishing boat that belonged to Simon Peter and his brother Andrew. The brothers were tired, having worked all night and caught nothing. They listened to Jesus speaking while they were cleaning their nets.

Andrew was a disciple of John the Baptist who followed Jesus after he heard John say, "Look, the Lamb of God." Andrew spent the afternoon in a meeting with Jesus and following their conversation, he immediately found his brother Simon and said, "We have found the Messiah (that is the Christ) and he brought him to Jesus" (John 1:40–42).

Both Andrew and Simon (later to be renamed Peter by Jesus) had a heart for God and understood that one day God would send His Son, the Messiah, to become the salvation of His people.

Luke 5:4–11 continues:

When he had finished speaking, he said to Simon, "Put out into deep water, and let down the nets for a catch."

Simon answered, "Master, we've worked hard all night and haven't caught anything. But because you say so, I will let down the nets."

When they had done so, they caught such a large number of fish that their nets began to break. So, they signaled their partners in the other boat to come and help them, and they came and filled both boats so full that they began to sink.

When Simon Peter saw this, he fell at Jesus' knees and said, "Go away from me, Lord; I am a sinful man!" For he and all his companions were astonished at the catch of fish they had taken, and so were James and John, the sons of Zebedee, Simon's partners.

Then Jesus said to Simon, "Don't be afraid; from now on you will fish for people." So, they pulled their boats up on shore, left everything and followed him *(NLT)*.

What kind of people is Jesus looking for to become His disciples/ leaders? This is a good checklist to determine how we measure up to Jesus's expectations:

A Heart for God

Andrew and Peter had a heart for God, meaning that they were looking for a closer relationship with Him.

Remain Teachable

They were teachable based on the trust that they believed they could have in Jesus. They saw almost immediately that Jesus had an interest in them and their well-being.

Demonstrate a Servant Heart

They were expert fishermen, but Jesus provided a catch that was far bigger than they had seen, which forced them to get help from their partners in the other boats. They wanted others to benefit from the abundance that Jesus had provided. This is evidence of a servant heart.

Ask for Forgiveness—Keep Short Accounts with God

Simon Peter recognized that he was unworthy to be with the Messiah because he was convicted of his own sin.

Walk by Faith in Order to Overcome Fear

This was the first time that Jesus would remind His disciples, "Don't be afraid." This encouragement was repeated numerous times over the next three years because Jesus knew that fear would take their focus off God and prevent them from receiving all that God had prepared for them, and through them, to future generations.

Expect Jesus to Fulfill His Purposes Through You

The fishermen left their boats to follow Jesus because they wanted to know more. They were inspired through this relatively brief encounter with Jesus, and they wanted to be part of His purposes, even though they didn't know what they were getting into at this point. They took a step of faith based on trust because they sensed the love that Jesus had for them.

It is no different today. Jesus is looking for the same kind of people who want to make a difference for Him. He does not necessarily want to take you out of your sphere of influence, but He does want you to represent Him within that influence.

When Jesus was with His disciples in the upper room as described in John 13, He shared one more time the key principle of leadership that allows us to build trust with others. *He washed the disciples' feet!* This was considered a demeaning task, worthy only for a servant in the employ of his master. Jesus did not separate people by belief or unbelief in who He was. He washed Judas's (the betrayer) feet along with the others as a reminder to us that we cannot separate people based on our natural bias—we must love and work with them all.

This is one of the most significant lessons from the life of Moses is his commitment to God's purpose. Despite the opposition from the people he was leading, and even from his brother Aaron and later his sister Miriam, he never failed to intercede for them before the Lord, even to the point of offering his own life if God would spare them.

Moses put aside his own interests for the sake of others, which God is asking us to do as well. It takes far more energy to serve others than what we are capable of doing alone. The good news is that Christ in us will not only provide the resources to meet the needs of others, but He gives us the energy to persevere as well.

The Apostle Paul in 1 Thessalonians 2:7–8 says it well:

> Just as a nursing mother cares for her children, so we cared for you. Because we loved you so much, we were delighted to share with you not only the gospel of God but our lives as well.

These people were strangers to Paul before he began to work with them and share the Gospel. As a result, their lives were changed, and their stories had an impact throughout the known world. He gave them everything he had in order to allow them to have the same kind of relationship that he enjoyed with Jesus. This is the result of becoming a servant leader, and the reward is stated by Paul in 1 Thessalonians 2:19–20 (emphasis mine):

> For what is our hope, our joy, or the crown in which we will glory in the presence of our Lord Jesus when he comes? **Is it not you? Indeed, you are our glory and joy.**

CHAPTER 18:

The Battle for Control

ONE OF THE THINGS THAT WE CAN learn about our human nature is that we love to be in control. We believe our security is based on it. It is imperative in our human nature to be able to explain everything in order for us to control it. The problem with this is that we have intellectual limitations that prevent us from understanding everything. This does not stop us from trying.

The world we live in demands control while our human nature is built for freedom, and this is the greatest battle that we face in life. We either agree to comply or fight to be free.

Laws were established in order to control our human nature. Why? Because the negative side of our human nature is capable of extreme evil. It began with God's laws as expressed through Moses, and it continues today in a variety of forms whether we live in a so-called democracy or in a dictatorship.

The motivation behind God's laws was designed to deal with the fundamental need of humanity, **the need to experience forgiveness**.

We were born with the need to be forgiven, inherited from Adam, and God's laws pointed us to the coming Messiah, who would take our sinful pride upon Himself and die on a cross in agony in order to set us free. He then sent us the gift of His Holy Spirit to place His laws on our hearts. Hebrews 10:16 says, "This is the covenant I will make with them after that time, says the Lord. I will put my laws in their hearts, and I will write them on their minds."

And the result, as it says in Galatians 5:1 is, "It is for freedom that Christ has set us free. Stand firm, then, and do not let yourselves be burdened again by a yoke of slavery."

So, ask yourself, are you free, or are you in bondage?

We are citizens of heaven, which requires us to live under the law of freedom, while at the same time we live on earth, which requires us to live within the laws of society that are imposed on us. Are these the only restraints that we impose upon ourselves? I don't think so.

The way we feel about ourselves can be a restraint if we are not happy with who we are. Insecure leaders are a danger to themselves and the people that report to them because their energy is focused internally on themselves rather than developing others.

Our own personality can be a restraint if it is used in a harmful manner. As a big P, your tendency might be to go through life telling people what to do according to the way you would do it, but that is not necessarily the best way to do it. Using your authority and telling people what to do is short-lived as a leadership tool, and, if overused, it can break a person's spirit.

If you are a big A style, you are driven to make decisions void of risk, which is very hard to do in a world that is constantly changing.

If you are a big E style, your self-worth is tied to your ideas, and you need the reinforcement of others in order to feel fulfilled. This style must be careful because the reinforcement you receive may not be genuine.

Finally, the big I's are motivated through unity, and they will try to achieve it at all costs, even making compromises that can be harmful in the long run. As Dr. Adizes says, "The appearance of consensus does not mean reality, wrong decisions can be made by consensus."[22] If you follow your natural tendencies, your personality does not give you the freedom to make good decisions on your own, and this is why we need others to offer different perspectives.

You begin to understand freedom when you allow others to think differently from you, and you take that into serious consideration when making decisions. These are the characteristics of a complementary team.

The constraints imposed on us through the laws of the land are not universal in their appreciation because what is good for one person can be seen as a restriction for another. The definition of what's best for humanity, the greater good, is used as a measuring device in creating policy, but this is really an interpretation based on a worldview that believes humans can control everything. Dissenting views are pushed aside, and, even within democracies, we fail to listen to one another.

We are expected to follow the rules that are imposed on us, even if they are contrary to our belief that God created us to achieve our full potential through the freedom that is offered in a relationship with Him. Being constrained by human beings feels very different that being restrained by God in order to be released to the fullness of life that He intends for us.

So, how do we compare the worldview with the plan that God has in store for us that we will experience in heaven and are training for here on earth?

Everything that God has done since the formation of the world and the creation of humankind has been done for our benefit. He created us in His image, which allows us, through the regeneration of Christ, to adopt His character and His holiness. The central characteristic of God's personality is love that is delivered to us through His servant heart. The key to believing this and accepting His grace comes through what the Bible calls obedience. The freedom that is ours from God is to accept His input or not. This is where the real challenge of living in two worlds comes in.

We have a new nature given to us the moment we were born again, and the old nature that we were born with and that still exists within us until we die. How can we bring clarity to this dilemma? It is important to realize that Jesus does not demand that we follow Him. We have the choice, as Christians, to accept His authority over us or not. It is only through a spirit of humility based on a knowledgeable trust that we will be obedient to what God is saying to us. It is often our own pride that prevents us from accepting God's grace and mercy, and if this is true for you, then you must accept the responsibility for the choices that you make.

If we become Christians at an early age or even as teenagers and young adults, there is a possibility that we will begin to allow spiritual ageing to enter our lives. This can happen for many reasons, some intentional, and others simply as a result of losing our focus on our relationship with God.

Some young people reject the faith of their parents because they find it too restrictive, or they believe it lacks practicality. I have news for you, allowing Christ into your life to guide you and to love you is the "coolest" thing you could do! Others go off to school and are influenced by a different faith or humanistic beliefs. Peer pressure and the temptations of life can cause spiritual decay. Faith in God has to be personal, real, and engaging. For that to happen it cannot be borrowed from someone else.

From my experience, Diagram 18.1 illustrates the most significant point of danger on our spiritual journey that will take our eyes off God. It is our drive to succeed from a worldly perspective, which I call the "Achieving" phase. When we get a little older, and are involved in raising a young family, trying to buy a house, and advancing in our careers, we find ourselves exhausted with very little time for church or having a devotional quiet time on a regular basis. Our default tendencies to depend on self or others rather than God will cause us to trust God less in our daily lives.

Diagram 18:1 Spiritual Decay

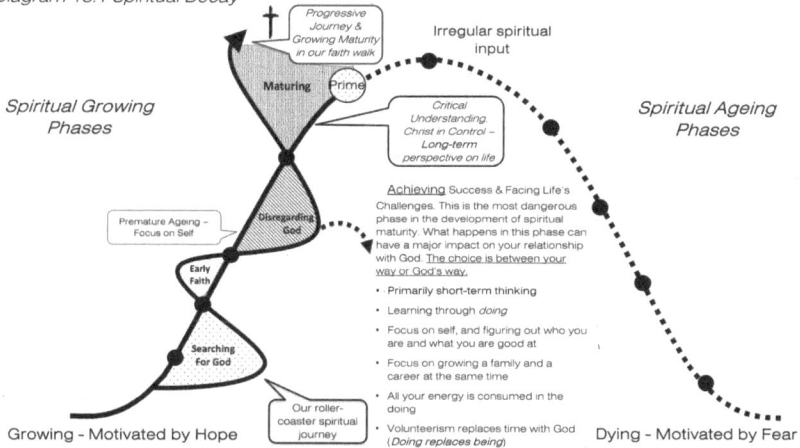

Spiritual Growing Phases

Progressive Journey & Growing Maturity in our faith walk

Maturing   Prime

Critical Understanding. Christ in Control – Long-term perspective on life

Irregular spiritual input

Spiritual Ageing Phases

Premature Ageing – Focus on Self

Disregarding God

Early Faith

Searching for God

Achieving Success & Facing Life's Challenges. This is the most dangerous phase in the development of spiritual maturity. What happens in this phase can have a major impact on your relationship with God. The choice is between your way or God's way.

• Primarily short-term thinking

• Learning through doing

• Focus on self, and figuring out who you are and what you are good at

• Focus on growing a family and a career at the same time

• All your energy is consumed in the doing

• Volunteerism replaces time with God (Doing replaces being)

Our roller-coaster spiritual journey

Growing - Motivated by Hope

Dying - Motivated by Fear

But we protest this idea because we have a life to live. "I have a business to run and people depending on me for their living; I have a family to take care of, and I am exhausted at the end of the day, and I don't have two minutes for myself; I have a dying Mom to look after; I work for the government and there are so many reports that I am responsible for."

The things that we think we can control are the things that will hold us back from seeking the Lord for His input.

Do you think God is unaware of your circumstance? Did His last command to us actually say, "Go into all the world, and I wish you the best of luck?"

Our tendency so often is to look at ourselves before we seek God's input. We look at our circumstances through the eyes of our old nature, which is designed to depend on self, and we soon discover that we face a number of very real limitations. The outcome is the realization that we are not really in control of our own lives.

I believe it is important for Christians to evaluate the condition of our faith journey with the Lord on a regular basis. We obviously did this at some point in our lives when we asked for forgiveness and were born again, but how is your relationship with Him today?

In 1 John 1:7 we are told,

> If we claim that we experience a shared life with him and continue to stumble around in the dark, we're obviously lying through our teeth—we're not living what we claim. But if we walk in the light, God himself being the light, we also experience a shared life with one another, as the sacrificed blood of Jesus, God's Son, purges all our sin *(The Message)*.

Or put another way in Proverbs 29:18, "If people can't see what God is doing, they stumble all over themselves; But when they attend to what He reveals, they are most blessed" *(The Message)*.

Or as the late Howie Hendricks used to say, "If you don't know where you ae going, any road will get you there!"[23]

The strength of your relationship with God will have a strong impact on how much you consult with Him when faced with difficult circumstances. He created your personality in the womb, He knew you before you were born, and He already knows the days that are ordained for you. Jesus Christ will give you His input based on who you are, what you are dealing with, and the wisdom He will offer for the needs at hand. All we have to do is ask.

Life is full of surprises, and not everything in life is planned. Sometimes events just happen, and we need wisdom to know which doors to walk through when they become available to us.

When I graduated from university, I wanted to be an urban planner. I had a degree in geography, and I was motivated by the spatial distribution of things in order to create an effective and efficient environment. I applied to thirty cities and towns seeking a position as an urban planner. I didn't ask the Lord about this idea because I was not yet a Christian. Even so, God knew me better than I knew myself, and

I realize now that His hand was on my life. I was turned down thirty times due to lack of experience in the field and not having a master's degree in the subject.

During this time, I was approached be a classmate who asked if I had ever thought about teaching at the high school level as Ontario, in 1967, was desperate for teachers. I discussed this with Wendy and responded to a newspaper ad to teach in Cornwall, Ontario, about sixty miles west of Montreal, where Wendy and I grew up and attended university. We had planned to get married in the summer of 1968 after she completed teacher's training in Quebec.

Within a period of about two weeks, I was interviewed and accepted a position to teach a full load of geography courses at Cornwall Collegiate and Vocational School. During the interview I was asked if I knew anyone else who would like to teach in Cornwall. I spoke to Wendy about it, then took her to be interviewed, and she accepted a position to teach English at a different high school in Cornwall. We would both be attending summer teacher's training for eight weeks at McArthur College, Queen's University, Kingston, Ontario.

Within a short period of time, life changed dramatically for both of us. In mid-June 1967, we were married and took a two-week camping honeymoon in New England before we truly began our married life in married students' quarters at McArthur College.

Looking back, I believe God was in control of our circumstances even before we realized what a born-again relationship with Him was all about. It was only later in life, as our faith matured, that we realized the opportunities available to us were orchestrated by God Himself. We learned to trust Him because we knew He had our best interests at heart.

Our lives in Christ are full of adventure and anticipation, as we expect God to show up in our daily routines, especially when we get into difficulty. Our role is to stay close to Him through our daily communication and our time in His Word. As Charles Spurgeon says, "We need the fresh oil of anointing from the Lord on a daily basis."[24] It takes discipline to keep this routine moving forward, but it is as essential as your morning coffee, your senior management meeting, taking the kids to school or picking them up, or any of the other priorities that you have on your list.

Please don't neglect meeting with other Christians and being free to share what God is doing in your life. Sharing with others is a form of ministry, encouragement, and growth. I have talked about the significance of the weekly Tuesday and Thursday mornings Zoom calls we call Bibles and Bros. and the inspiration that we receive as each one has a chance to share. The impact widens our perspective of what God is doing and how we can have a ministry in each other's lives.

Finally, I encourage you to seek God before you seek anyone else. Share your dreams, your ideas, and your love for Him. Talk to Him about the people who are on your mind constantly and pray for them, especially your family and the people you work with. Ask God to allow you to serve them as only God can, through His Spirit. We all need encouragement. Ask Him to show you how to encourage others today. You will be the giver of God's blessings and in turn you will receive His blessing.

The words of the Apostle Paul in Romans 12:1–2 are a fitting challenge to us as we contemplate the future:

> So, here's what I want you to do, God helping you: Take your everyday, ordinary life—your sleeping, eating, going-to-work, and walking-around life—and place it before God as an offering. Embracing what God does for you is the best thing you can do for him. Don't become so well-adjusted to your culture that you fit into it without even thinking. Instead, fix your attention on God. You'll be changed from the inside out. Readily recognize what he wants from you, and quickly respond to it. Unlike the culture around you,

always dragging you down to its level of immaturity, God brings the best out of you, develops well-formed maturity in you *(The Message)*.

Let go of the controls and let God guide your life and show you how to use the gifts that He has equipped you with, and begin with the people who are within your sphere of influence. These are the lessons that Moses learned through his daily walk with God, and as His humble servant, he became known as the greatest leader who ever lived.

If you are reading this book and you are uncertain about your relationship with God, His Word says, "For this is how God loved the world: He gave his one and only Son, so that **everyone who believes in him** will not perish but have eternal life (*LB*, John 3:16, emphasis mine).

You can begin by asking God to help you to believe that Jesus loves you and wants you to have a relationship with Him. Once you believe, God's Holy Spirit will tell what to do next in order for you to begin your journey with Him.

God bless you as you walk with Him.

APPENDIX

Evaluating Your Management Style

The attached material is a non-scientific evaluation of your personality based on my observations of the behaviour of people observed over the past fifty-five years. The statements that you read on the attached forms are characteristics defined by the four roles of management that was discussed in the book in Chapter 2. There are twelve statements for each role describing the P, Producer role, the A, Administrator role, the E, Entrepreneurial role, and the I, Integrator role. The statements are all mixed up so that you can determine which ones are the real you! The instructions are found below.

Before you begin:

1. In what frame of mind should you be in when you read the statements and circle the ones that you believe are you? First, you need to be relaxed! Don't do this if you have an immediate deadline to meet.

2. Do not fill this out based on what is expected from you at work. If you answer based on work expectations, it is often what you believe is expected from you, which may not be a correct evaluation of who you are or what you really enjoy doing. Answer from the perspective of who you are, not what you *want* to be or *should* be. See the description of IS, WANT, and SHOULD on page 106.

3. Read the statements and ask yourself, "Is this the real me? Do I really enjoy or am I good at doing the things that the statements are suggesting?"

How to use the forms to determine your management style:

1. **Form #1** is the first one to fill out. There are forty-eight statements. **Circle only those that you believe are the real you.**

2. If possible, check your answers from **Form #1** with someone who knows you well. Listen to their input and make adjustments to your answers if necessary.

3. Then transfer the answers to **Form #2** by **circling the P, A, E, and I letters** that correspond to the numbers on **Form #1** that you circled. Then add up the number of P's, A's, E's, and I's and place the numbers at the bottom of **Form #2** in the place provided at the bottom.

4. Plot the numbers on the graph in the appropriate quadrant:

   P = Producer, A = Administrator, E = Entrepreneur, and I = Integrator and connect the dots.

   Take the PAEI numbers from the box at the bottom of **Form #2** on the score sheet and place a dot on the graph in the appropriate box for the Producer, Administrator, Entrepreneur, and Integrator. There may be some answers reflecting eleven or twelve choices. Simply place those numbers slightly above #10 on the appropriate line.

Connect the dots by joining them like the example on page 15. The graph will show you your management style strengths based on the four roles. It will also show you which management roles are not your strengths based on the lower value numbers.

5. A sample graph is found on page 15 in the book.

6. There are no wrong answers. Your value is not found in how big each letter is! Enjoy finding out your management style. Make note of the combination letters in your style. Look for the largest letters in the four and determine you default behavioural characteristics from the descriptions on pages 14–19

Form #1 Management Style Questionnaire

Instructions: Setting: Relax, in your favorite chair thinking about the real you. Circle the numbers of the statements that generally describe you. Go with your first instinct.

No.	Work Habit
1	I am great at getting things organized and putting processes and systems into place.
2	I do not enjoy doing the same things over and over.
3	I can read the unspoken undertones and know what people are really thinking.
4	I believe it is important to slow down and think things through.
5	I don't like to be overly managed but I do think it is important to be accountable
6	I am great at putting out fires and quickly responding to a crisis.
7	In a meeting, I generally like to hear what others have to say before I share my thoughts.
8	I generally agree that if you can't measure something, you can't manage it.
9	I need some freedom to make decisions.
10	I work on teams, but the truth is that I prefer to work on my own.
11	I enjoy helping others to complete a task
12	My work days are very organized and I don't like to be disturbed
13	I make quite a few decisions based on intuition and gut instinct.
14	I appreciate people who work hard and are passionate about their work
15	The work environment is important to me.
16	I keep my work area neat and well-organized.
17	New ideas and new projects are what get me excited.
18	I have a tendency to overcommit; I have difficulty saying "no" when people ask me to do something.
19	I prefer to make decisions after talking things over with trusted members of my team.
20	I like to know the facts before I open my mouth.
21	When I say "yes" to an idea, it often means "maybe" because I can change my mind later.
22	I like to be recognized for all the hard work I do.
23	Sometimes I just let others have their way instead of arguing with them.
24	I like to make important decisions thoughtfully and carefully weigh all options.
25	A lot of my meetings happen on the spur of the moment.
26	I like to plunge in, just figure stuff out rather than spend a lot of time talking about it.
27	I enjoy working with people more than I enjoy working alone.
28	I prefer meetings that are well organized with agendas and follow-up actions.
29	I can keep track of things in my head; I don't need to write everything down.
30	I often find that to do the job right, it is easier to do it myself.
31	I can have difficulty making decisions especially if someone I care about disagrees.
32	If I don' think there is enough information, I have no problem saying "no" to a half-baked idea.
33	I spend a fair amount of time thinking about the future and where things are going.
34	It seems like I always have too much to do; there just isn't enough time to get it all done.
35	I like to take the time to get know the people I work with.
36	I enjoy solving complex problems that require a lot of thought.
37	I get upset when people criticize my ideas.
38	My workspace may look disorganized but I know where everything is.
39	I feel good about who I am and I am not afraid to take responsibility when things don't go well.
40	Silence does not mean agreement to me; it means I am thinking.
41	Once I get something figured out, I like to move on to something new.
42	I am generally quick to respond to situations.
43	I believe it is really important to get ideas from others before we make a final decision
44	I think it is important to develop a detailed plan before we jump into action.
45	I like to give the team credit for things well done.
46	I am often one of the earliest to get to work and one of the last to leave.
47	I'm not big on small talk; I prefer to get right to the point!
48	I am great at seeing things others do not, and coming up with clever new ways to do things.

Form #2: Management Style Score Sheet

Instructions: Circle the numbers of the statements from your assessment worksheet on the score sheet. Place the PAEI numbers in the box below.

#	Style	Work Habit
1	A	I am great at getting things organized and putting processes and systems into place.
2	E	I do not enjoy doing the same things over and over.
3	I	I can read the unspoken undertones and know what people are really thinking.
4	A	I believe it is important to slow down and think things through.
5	E	I don't like to be overly managed but I do think it is important to be accountable
6	P	I am great at putting out fires and quickly responding to a crisis.
7	I	In a meeting, I generally like to hear what others have to say before I share my thoughts.
8	A	I generally agree that if you can't measure something, you can't manage it.
9	E	I need some freedom to make decisions.
10	P	I work on teams, but the truth is that I prefer to work on my own.
11	I	I enjoy helping others to complete a task
12	A	My work days are very organized and I don't like to be disturbed
13	E	I make quite a few decisions based on intuition and gut instinct.
14	P	I appreciate people who work hard and are passionate about their work
15	I	The work environment is important to me.
16	A	I keep my work area neat and well-organized.
17	E	New ideas and new projects are what get me excited.
18	P	I have a tendency to overcommit; I have difficulty saying "no" when people ask me to do
19	I	I prefer to make decisions after talking things over with trusted members of my team.
20	A	I like to know the facts before I open my mouth.
21	E	When I say "yes" to an idea, it often means "maybe" because I can change my mind later.
22	P	I like to be recognized for all the hard work I do.
23	I	Sometimes I just let others have their way instead of arguing with them.
24	A	I like to make important decisions thoughtfully and carefully weigh all options.
25	E	A lot of my meetings happen on the spur of the moment.
26	P	I like to plunge in, just figure stuff out rather than spend a lot of time talking about it.
27	I	I enjoy working with people more than I enjoy working alone.
28	A	I prefer meetings that are well organized with agendas and follow-up actions.
29	E	I can keep track of things in my head; I don't need to write everything down.
30	P	I often find that to do the job right, it is easier to do it myself.
31	I	I can have difficulty making decisions especially if someone I care about disagrees.
32	A	If I don't think there is enough information, I have no problem saying "no" to a half-baked idea.
33	E	I spend a fair amount of time thinking about the future and where things are going.
34	P	It seems like I always have too much to do; there just isn't enough time to get it all done.
35	I	I like to take the time to get know the people I work with.
36	A	I enjoy solving complex problems that require a lot of thought.
37	E	I get upset when people criticize my ideas.
38	P	My workspace may look disorganized but I know where everything is.
39	I	I feel good about who I am and I am not afraid to take responsibility when things don't go well.
40	A	Silence does not mean agreement to me; it means I am thinking.
41	E	Once I get something figured out, I like to move on to something new.
42	P	I am generally quick to respond to situations.
43	I	I believe it is really important to get ideas from others before we make a final decision
44	A	I think it is important to develop a detailed plan before we jump into action.
45	I	I like to give the team credit for things well done.
46	P	I am often one of the earliest to get to work and one of the last to leave.
47	P	I'm not big on small talk; I prefer to get right to the point!
48	E	I am great at seeing things others do not, and coming up with clever new ways to do things.

"P" number = _____ "A" number = _____ "E" number = _____ "I" number = _____

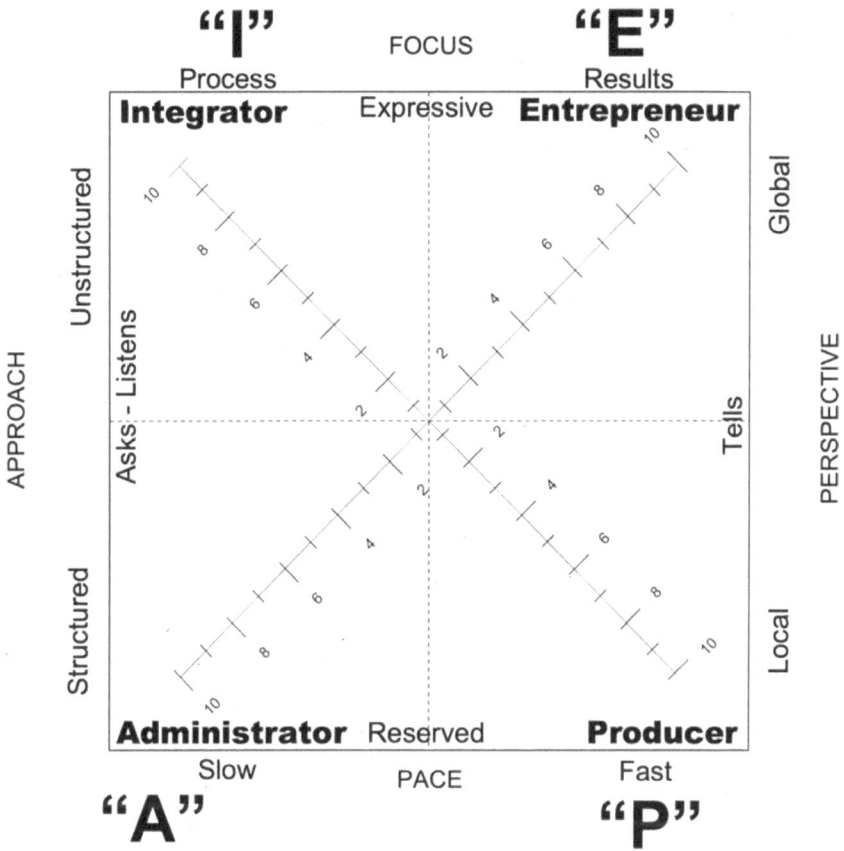

RECOMMENDATIONS

There are several Bibles and devotional books I want to refer to that guide my relationship with the Lord, and I use them every day to gain insight, journaling the thoughts that are significant for me.

- *The Holy Bible, New International Version.* Zondervan Corp., 2005. This is God's Word, and He speaks to me through the chapters that I read every day.

- Peterson, Eugene H. *The Message; The Bible in Contemporary Language,* Nav Press, 2002.

- *The Leadership Bible, NIV.* Zondervan Corp., 1998.

- *The Amplified Bible,* The Lockman Foundation, 2002.

- *The New Living Translation.* Tyndale House Publishers, *1996.*

- Chambers, Oswald. *My Utmost for His Highest,* Discovery House, 1963. This is really an encouragement to walk with the Lord daily, looking deeply into my heart to impart Biblical truth.

- Maxell, John. *Leadership Promises for Every Day*, J. Countryman, a division of Thomas Nelson, Inc., 2003. I have learned so much from John Maxwell through this daily devotional, and I have tried to apply every aspect of his biblically-based wisdom through my leadership responsibilities.

- Swindoll, Charles. *Wisdom for the Way*, J. Countryman, a division of Thomas Nelson, Inc., 2001. The Bible is full of the wisdom of the Lord, and Charles Swindoll has helped to apply that wisdom to my everyday experience.

- Spurgeon, Charles H., revised and updated by Alistair Begg. *Morning and Evening*, Crossway, Wheaton, Illinois.

In addition to the above, I would like to pay a special tribute to the late Dr. William R. Bright, whose writings, teaching, and modelling are the foundation of our understanding of what it means to walk by faith. His writings live on in the following three references that made a significant difference in our lives:

- *The Ten Basic Steps Toward Christian Maturity*, New Life Publishing, 2002.

- *How to Experience God's Love and Forgiveness*, New Life Publishing, 2002.

- *The Holy Spirit: The Key to Supernatural Living*, New Life Publishing, 2002.

Several Books written by Dr. Ichak Adizes and the training offered by the Adizes Institute have been especially meaningful in my development as a leader. Published by the Adizes Institute Publications, the most influential for me have been:

- *Managing Corporate Lifecycles*

- *Mastering Change*

- *Leading the Leaders*

- *Management/Mismanagement Styles*

- *The Ideal Executive*

Previous Books by Barry Bowater

- *The Prime of My Life, Finding Joy in the Journey*, 2019.
  Freedom to Live, Courage to Lead, 2021.

ENDNOTES

Chapter 2: Why Are We Lost?

1   "Who do we have faith in? The world's most trusted professions." Ipsos.com survey 2019.

2   Chambers, Oswald. *My Utmost for His Highest*, Oswald Chambers Publications Association Ltd., 1992. (Updated Edition, Edited by James Reimann).

3   Adizes, Ichak. *Leading the Leaders*, The Adizes Institute, 2004, Chapter Two.

Chapter 4: Overcoming Barriers to Success

4   Maxwell, John. *Leadership Promises for Every Day*, J. Countryman, a Division of Thomas Nelson, Inc., 2003, p. 142.

Chapter 5: Without Faith It Is Impossible to Please God

5   Chambers, May 9.

6   Historical maps provided courtesy of Headwaters Christian Resources.

Chapter 7: Serving Others–The Foundation of Leadership

7   Adizes, Ichak. *Management and Mismanagement Styles*, The Adizes Institute, 2004, p. 150.

Chapter 8: Building a Foundation of Trust

8   Maxwell, p. 218.

Chapter 11: Leadership Is Complicated

9   Maxwell, p. 113.

10   *The Leadership Bible, NIV*. Zondervan Publishing House, 1998, p. 1.

11   *The Leadership Bible. NIV*, p. 69.

12   *The Leadership Bible. NIV*, p. 119.

13   *The Leadership Bible. NIV*, p. 151.

14   *The Leadership Bible. NIV*, p. 198.

15   Hendricks, Howard. "The Role of the Pastor" video.

Chapter 15: The Spontaneous Impact of Discipline

16   Adizes, Ichak. *Mastering Change,* The Adizes Institute, 1992, p. 161–180.

17   *Mastering Change.*

18   Maxwell, p. 185.

Chapter 16: The Courage to Confront

19   Maxwell, p. 231.

Chapter 17: Called to Serve in Times of Change

20   Maxwell, p. 207.

21   Swindoll, p. 212.

Chapter 18: The Battle for Control

22   Adizes, *Management and Mismanagement Styles,* p. 162.

23   "The Role of the Pastor."

24   Spurgeon, Charles. *Morning and Evening,* Crossway, revised and
      updated by Alistair Begg, 2003, July 16.

Printed in Canada